BECOMING *a*
WOMAN
of the
WORD

KAROL LADD

HARVEST HOUSE PUBLISHERS
EUGENE, OREGON

Cover by Harvest House Publishers, Eugene, Oregon

Cover photo © funky-data / Vetta / iStock

Karol Ladd is published in association with the literary agency of the Steve Laube Agency, LLC, 5025 N. Central Ave., #635, Phoenix, Arizona, 85012.

BECOMING A WOMAN OF THE WORD

Copyright © 2014 by Karol Ladd
Published by Harvest House Publishers
Eugene, Oregon 97402
www.harvesthousepublishers.com

Library of Congress Cataloging-in-Publication Data
Ladd, Karol.
Becoming a woman of the word / Karol Ladd.
pages cm
ISBN 978-0-7369-5804-2 (pbk.)
ISBN 978-0-7369-5805-9 (eBook)
1. Bible—Introductions. 2. Christian women—Religious life. I. Title.
BS475.3.L33 2014
220.6'1082—dc23

2014005156

Printed in the United States of America

14 15 16 17 18 19 20 21 22 / VP-JH / 10 9 8 7 6 5 4 3 2 1

To every woman who dares to
discover the power of God's Word to transform her daily life.

Acknowledgments

Thank you to the tremendous Harvest House team. Bob, LaRae, Brad, Shane, Paul, Barb, and the entire staff, I'm grateful for your vision for this book and for your enthusiastic effort to get it in the hands of women who desire to "Grow True." Thank you to my literary agent, Steve Laube, for your heart for Christ and your desire to further God's kingdom through great books. Thank you to Tammy, Becky, Cathy, Julie, Amy, and Leslie for your constant desire to serve Him and for your help and encouragement to me.

Contents

Anything but Boring

Heaven and earth will pass away, but my words will not pass away.

MATTHEW 24:35

We can never exhaust all the treasure and worth that is in the Word.

THOMAS MANTON

*W*here are you with the Bible? Perhaps you've tried to read it and just haven't connected with it. Or maybe you simply didn't know where to start. On the other hand, you could be that person who has gone to Bible studies for years, and yet your interest in it has grown a little stale. Perhaps you've never had any interest in it at all. When it comes to the Bible, we are all at different places. No matter where you are, my hope is that this book will bring you to a place of connection—connecting your life with the greatest book that has ever been written.

I was first introduced to the Bible when I was a little girl living in Detroit, Michigan. Yes, it was very cold (the weather, not the Bible). We went to a church in downtown Detroit, where our car was broken into more than once while we were attending services. The thing I remember most about the church was not the break-ins, but rather the kindness of our Sunday school teacher, who gave us Bibles and taught us how to look up passages in the Holy Scriptures. She led me to memorize Psalm 23, even though the Bible was completely new to me. This teacher sparked a love in me for the Bible and ignited a desire to get to know this sacred book.

As I grew through my teenage years, I found great comfort in the Scriptures to help me weather the storms of life and the breakups with boyfriends. As I went to college, the Bible gave me hearty doses of wisdom and direction in daily living. When I got married it became my companion in working through relationship and communication issues. It taught me that God understood my feelings even when my husband didn't! As a young mom, the Scriptures reminded me that God was my strength and would give me everything I needed. It taught me to not worry, but rather in a very real way to cast my cares on the Lord. There were also times when I felt distant from God's Word as the busyness of life choked out my interest. Yet, as I look back over my life as a whole, the Bible has been my steady guide, teaching me about God's unfailing love for me.

There are some people who may think the Bible is irrelevant or doesn't pertain to our lives today, but I'm pretty sure those people haven't read it! What could be more relevant than a book filled with stories of people from a variety of backgrounds and experiences, all reflecting the human condition and the desperate need inside each of us for love and redemption? The beautiful theme throughout the entire book is not how bad *we* are, but how good *God* is. Every page is infused with His grace.

The Bible is a book about messed-up lives and God's unmerited favor. There is no other book on earth that conveys the abiding love of Almighty God toward His people. Why wouldn't you want to read a book like that? Throughout the centuries it has given strength and inspiration to artists, businesspeople, authors, musicians, athletes, and world leaders. It has offered hope to the ailing in hospitals, to the suffering on the battle-fields, and to the starving in poverty.

To be honest, though, true poverty is the "poverty of the soul."

How sad to have all the comforts that life can offer, yet be empty or starved spiritually. The Bible is food to feed our hungry hearts, bringing fulfillment and nourishment to our soul. This is why we read it—because, like food, we need it for our very existence. It is filled with life-giving sustenance for those who hunger to know God's grace and love. Cultural blogger Jim Denison wrote, "This hunger for the God of grace is universal. How could it not be? We were designed to need food, and will hunger for it until the day we die. In the same way, we were designed to need our Designer."[1] Yes, "Man does not live on bread alone but on every word that comes from the mouth of the LORD" (Deuteronomy 8:3).

The Journey Begins

Just so you know, I have never gone to seminary, nor did I get my degree in biblical studies. I'm just a normal girl who loves the adventure of learning great truths from God's Word, and I want to invite you on the journey as well. The Bible is filled with history, poetry, prophecy, wisdom, letters, and most importantly, the story of Jesus. It's anything but boring! Through the pages in this book, I hope to light a fire of fascination and delight in your heart for the wonderful Word of God.

Becoming a Woman of the Word is broken down into four parts. We start off with practical ways to get to know the Bible through reading it, studying it, and meditating on it. The second part is all about encouraging your love for the Scriptures by showing you the big picture of the Bible and introducing you to several themes throughout it. The third part focuses on applying biblical truths to your daily life, examining topics such as prayer, compassion, and worship. The final part is a bonus section, which I call "Good to Know." It's filled with helpful information about how we got the Bible, choosing a translation, and where to find certain passages.

At the end of each chapter, I've added a section called "Digging Deeper" so you can take what you've learned and explore God's Word a little further if you like. I encourage you to purchase a journal to use as you walk through this book with me in order for you to record what you learn in the "Digging Deeper" sections. You can use this book as a group study or as a personal journey. I've added discussion questions at the end of each chapter, and I've also provided a guide at the back of the book to help you break the book down into a six-, seven-, or eight-week group study.

Finally (and I'm so excited about this!), you will find a 22-Day Challenge in the back of the book. Why 22? Because that's how many letters are in the Hebrew alphabet. Now don't worry, we are not going to study the Hebrew alphabet. The real reason behind the 22-Day Challenge is that there is a wonderful psalm in the Bible, Psalm 119, which is broken down into 22 sections. The psalmists used the Hebrew alphabet to create one of the most poetic psalms in the Bible, extolling the beauty of God's Word. I want you to get to know this psalm as a fellow lover of God's Word. This delightful challenge invites you to read a short section of Psalm 119 each day and consider its truths. My hope is that as you take this challenge, you will catch the passion of the psalmists and grow to delight in the Word in an even deeper way than you have ever experienced before in your life.

Do you believe the Bible contains everything a person needs to live a meaningful life? If it is our one main objective source of all the revelation God has given us about Himself and His plan for humanity, then we ought to dig deep into this amazing and powerful book. My prayer is that God will use *Becoming a Woman of the Word* to not only help you get to know the Bible, but also to rely upon His Word as your essential resource for daily living. May you find the true refreshment of knowing you are sincerely loved by Almighty God.

I adore the fullness of the Scriptures.

TERTULLIAN

Part One

Knowing the Bible

~

Guide me in your truth and teach me,
for you are God my Savior,
and my hope is in you all day long.

PSALM 25:5

The Bible:
Read it to get the facts,
study it to get the meaning,
meditate on it to get the benefit.

DAVID SHEPHERD

The Bible is a life-changing book, relationally rich and powerfully transforming. (Doesn't that sound like God Himself?) These next few chapters are intended to help you to make a personal connection with the Word of God. My heart's desire is that you will find great delight in opening up the Bible and getting to know it in a way you never have before. Knowing the Bible is much more than just reading words on the page—it is engaging with it and allowing it to permeate your life. Ultimately, part 1 is all about opening up the door to allow your life to intersect with the God of the Bible. As you get to know His Word, you get to know Him.

We begin with the "Invitation to Dine," recognizing the value and joy of spending some still, quiet moments with Him. I introduce the next chapter with the title "Daily Swim," which describes the refreshing and invigorating practice of reading His Word each day. "Diving Deeper" equips you to do your own treasure hunt when you study the Bible for yourself, and "Breathing It In" leads you to meditate on the Scriptures. Finally, I share my own practical and doable tips on memorizing Scripture in the chapter "Never Go Anywhere Without It."

May God use each of these chapters to bolster your understanding and increase your confidence as you come to know the Bible, and God Himself, in a deeper and richer way.

1

Invitation to Dine

Show me your ways, LORD,
teach me your paths.

PSALM 25:4

The Bible is alive, it speaks to me; it has feet, it runs after me;
it has hands, it lays hold on me.

MARTIN LUTHER

Our electricity seems to go out at the most inconvenient moments. For example, one time I was hopping out of the shower with sopping wet hair, and all of a sudden everything went dark—no lights and no blow dryer. That's never a good start to the day! Recently, I was working furiously to finish writing a book with the deadline fast approaching, and the lights began to flicker. You guessed it, yet again the faulty transformer in our neighborhood was on the blink, and the electricity was completely out for blocks. This time, I packed up my bags and headed out the door (fortunately my car wasn't in the garage since the electric garage door didn't work either). I knew I needed to find a place that had accessible electric plugs and wireless Internet, and I needed to find it quick!

That day a quaint local bakery became my makeshift office for the next several hours while I waited for the electricity to return. I watched the breakfast crowd dwindle and the lunch crowd emerge as I typed away at my little table while munching on a cranberry muffin (or two). The early lunchers had their pick of tables, and I must admit I got distracted by all the activity as people claimed their tables. An elderly man and his grown daughter chose the table next to mine. Something about the sweetness of their relationship grabbed my interest. The daughter lovingly cared for her father and made sure he was comfortable and taken care of. She went and got their food, brought it to the table, and then they just sat together eating their lunch, not saying a word, simply enjoying each other's company.

It was truly a tender scene to me—father and daughter together, relishing each other's presence. I could easily see that they valued their time together. The father loved being with his daughter, while the daughter seemed to count it a privilege to have time with her daddy. They weren't rushed. They didn't have an agenda. They were simply together. It occurred to me that this scene reflected the beauty of God's invitation to us, His daughters, to simply be together and spend time with Him. What peace comes from setting aside everything else and simply being still, communing with our loving Father. We need it. The busyness and distractions of life can tend to stress us and frazzle us, but a quiet and still time with our patient and gentle heavenly Father can bring order and strength to our hurried lives.

As much as we may value and long for time alone with Almighty God, the thing that boggles my mind is the fact that He desires to fellowship with us as well. That's amazing! How can it be that holy God desires to abide with us? It comes down to one word—*love*. He is love. His very essence is love and He chooses to lavish His love on us, His children. The Bible reminds us, "As a father has compassion on his children, so the Lord has compassion on those who fear him" (Psalm 103:13). As believers in Christ, we are His precious possession, His daughters, His family. As with the sweet scene of the daughter and father dining together at the bakery, so our Father invites us to come, be still, and dine with Him.

The Power of the Family Dinner

When my kids were young, I tried to make dinnertime around the table a priority, but it wasn't easy. Between soccer practice and gymnastics and homework, it was hard to bring everyone together at the table. Yet, recent studies reveal that having dinner together as a family at least four times a week has a positive effect on a child's development. A consistent family dinnertime has been linked to lower risk of obesity, substance abuse, and eating disorders, and an increased chance of graduating from high school. Time around the table together not only provides an opportunity for conversation, but it also bolsters a sense of security and togetherness. Studies also show that children who eat dinner with their family are more likely to understand, acknowledge, and follow the boundaries and expectations set by their parents.[1]

Now if we can see the benefits of time around the dinner table together as a family, how much more is our life enriched as we sit at the table of our heavenly Father? Dining with Him and enjoying the rich nourishment from His word will not only give us a sense of security and togetherness, but will also make us more aware of His direction and desires for our lives. Spending time with our Father develops a deeper and richer relationship with Him and helps us in relating to others as well. Whether we are talking about family dinners or focused time with our heavenly Father, it begins with a decision, recognizing that this time is important enough in my life that I will make every effort to make it happen.

It's easy to become content with being "lukewarm" in our spiritual lives and actions. Instead of seeing our need for Him, we try to work it out ourselves and blow through our day in our own strength. It's interesting that Jesus addressed this very tendency in the book of Revelation. He said He would rather us be hot or cold than to be "lukewarm." And then He added the antidote to spiritual lukewarmness, "I stand at the door and knock. If anyone hears my voice and opens the door, I will come in and eat with that person, and they with me" (Revelation 3:20). It's not just an antidote; it's an invitation. God wants us to fellowship with Him, to dine with Him and commune with Him. Our part is to listen to His voice, open the door, and spend time with Him. This is how we guard against being lukewarm, and are empowered to live a vibrant and meaningful life.

As we abide with Him, we find strength and guidance. We experience a peace that passes all understanding as we give our cares and worries to Him. We gain a new perspective on life as we thank Him and praise Him for all He has done and will do and is doing in our lives. God has wired us in such a way that we find our soul's refreshment from our fellowship with Him. As a father has compassion on his children, so our Father has compassion on us. He welcomes us into His loving embrace each day. How can we not accept the invitation to sit at the table with Him?

A Time and a Place

The kitchen table is the place for family dinners. This is where family fellowship happens. The family knows when it is time to eat the evening meal; there is a consistent place to gather. Have you found a good place to meet and commune with the Lord? My friend Jody has a favorite cozy chair, which faces her backyard. She keeps her Bible and devotionals in a basket right by the chair, so she has her tools there at hand to dig into His Word. Another friend, Amy, uses a basket with a handle so she can carry her Bible and devotionals out to the back porch on a nice day or over to the couch on a rainy one. Often I begin my day at the kitchen table reading His Word, then for prayer I move to the atrium—my favorite spot in my house. The reason I like this spot is that is has a skylight in the ceiling, and I'm able to look up and see the heavens as I spend time with the Father. Where is a place that you can call your own, where you can meet with God each day? It may be the kitchen table or the living room couch or even a spare bedroom. Just as we come and dine at the same table with our family, there is comfort and consistency in finding a regular place to meet with God.

Throughout Scripture we find that God gave physical places spiritual significance. Jerusalem, the Jordan River, Bethel are just a few of the significant locations we find in Scripture. Consider the location you choose for your quiet time as sacred territory, a place where you meet God. It too will become a place of spiritual significance as you draw close in your love relationship with Him. I know certain married couples who have that spot where they first kissed or where he proposed or where they went on their first date. We too can have that spot with the Lover of our souls. He longs to speak His love into us in that place.

Consistency is helpful in both location and time of day. It has become my habit over the years the start the day off early with a time alone with the Lord. I want to meet with Him before I meet with anyone else. I like having my time early, as it sets the tone and prepares me to face the challenges of the day. For other people early morning just doesn't work. Take Julie for instance. She is required to be at work at 5:00 a.m. several days a week. She can barely get her shower in, much less have a quiet time in the morning. She has found that her best time to sit and be still with God is in the afternoon when she comes home from work and no one is around. On the other hand, take a mom like Shelly. It's all she can do to get her three kids off to school in the morning, so her favorite time with the Lord is mid-morning after she drops the kids off at school.

Stop right now and consider: What is the best time and the best place for you to come to the table and feast on the rich food of God's Word and enjoy His presence? Take a moment right now to pray and ask the Lord to help you figure out a consistent time and place. Don't worry about how everyone else does it; figure out what works for you. We must be intentional about it, or it simply won't happen. Write your decision on the lines below:

Time: _____

Place: _____

Now honestly, I know that life happens and there will be days that you just can't get there. Don't beat yourself up—God is not mad at you, I promise! He loves you and His invitation is simply and lovingly, "Come." He invites you with no strings attached because He knows that this time is for you to be blessed, not for you to feel condemned if you don't show up. May I encourage you to ask Him to help you stay consistent? Sometimes it even helps to have a friend, someone you challenge and who challenges you to stay consistent. For instance, recently I did a 40-day prayer challenge using a book about prayer. The fun part was, I did it with a friend, so we read the passage from the book each day and then e-mailed each other a simple sentence or two about what we learned from the reading for that day. It motivated me to keep consistent and not miss a day of the challenge.

Dining with Delight

Now that you have a time and place—what do you do? Where do you begin? Perhaps the ole point-a-finger-in-the-middle-of-the-Bible-and-read-a-verse-for-that-day strategy just isn't working for you. Let's consider ways to come and dine with the Father who loves you. There's no perfect routine or formula when it comes to spending time with God. For me, I start off each morning with my journal, my iPad (because my daily Bible reading and devotionals are on it), and of course a cup of coffee. I simply just sit still before God.

In my journal, I always begin by writing out at least five things I am thankful for from the past day. Of course, I usually end up writing much more than simply five things as I begin to recognize all the ways God has blessed me. I also deliberately thank the Lord for at least one challenge in my life as I consider what He is teaching me through the difficulty. And I can sincerely thank Him for His presence and peace as I walk through those challenges. Another habit I have started is to thank the Lord for at least one thing about my husband each day, because it keeps me focused on his positive qualities. And that's always a good thing!

After I spend time thanking the Lord then I open up His Word for a time of reading. He has given us His Spirit to lead us into all truth, so I begin by seeking His guidance. I invite His Spirit to be my teacher and open my eyes to new truths. Spiritual truth must be spiritually discerned, and we need God's Spirit to lead us. I like what author Andrew Murray (1828–1917) wrote about the importance of encountering God's Word with the help and guidance of the Holy Spirit:

> We must refuse to deal with the written Word without the quickening Spirit. Let us never take Scripture into our hand, mind, or mouth without realizing the need and the promise of the Spirit. First in a quiet act of worship, look to God to give and renew the working of His Spirit within you. Then, in a quiet act of faith, yield yourself to the power that dwells in you. Then wait on Him so that not only the mind, but the life in you, may be opened to receive the Word. The words of Christ are indeed Spirit and life.

Murray added this prayer:

> Lord God, I thank You again for the wonderful gift of the indwelling Spirit. Father, give me the Spirit of wisdom. May I know how deeply spiritual each word of Yours is, and may I know that spiritual things can only be spiritually discerned. Teach me in all my contact with Your Word to deny the flesh and the fleshly mind and to wait in deep humility and faith for the inward working of the Spirit to quicken the Word. May my meditation on Your Word, my keeping of it in faith and obedience, be in Spirit and in truth, in the life and in power. Amen.[2]

During my quiet time with the Lord, I use the *One Year Bible*, which offers a daily Bible reading with an entry from the Old Testament, New Testament, Psalms, and Proverbs, each in a doable dose. Many women— and men—have also found *The Daily Bible* to be a great resource because it arranges the Bible text in the order of the events that happened.* (I'll go into more about different options for reading your Bible in the next chapter.) This daily time of meeting with God is a time to read and meditate on the Bible and pray. You may choose other times throughout your week to study and dig into the Bible (which we will cover in chapter 3), but for a time of regular reflection and daily growth, I encourage you to simply read and meditate on His Word.

I also enjoy reading a devotional in addition to reading from His Word. Devotionals should not replace reading the Bible, but they can supplement your quiet time. Most devotionals take a verse and expand on it with the author's perspective or thoughts. At the end of this chapter, I've listed some of my favorite devotionals. At times, I may use a book with short chapters as a part of my devotional reading, such as *The Knowledge of the Holy* by A.W. Tozer, or *The Names of Jesus* by A.B. Simpson, or *The Spirit of Christ* by Andrew Murray, or *Here and Now* by Henri J.M. Nouwen. It is a healthy practice to journal and write out what God is teaching you so that you can reflect on it again or simply to help you identify and remember what you learned.

After a time of reading, I sit still and simply relax in His presence. I may go to the atrium and slip to my knees and praise and adore Him for who He is. I reflect on some of His qualities I've learned about in His Word or in the devotional reading, and I glorify His name. After praising Him for His wonderful attributes, I humbly recognize my own sin, so I spend time confessing and opening up my heart before Him. Again, I'm still and allow His Spirit to remind me of anything I need to confess that was not pleasing to Him. After confessing, I honestly can't help but thank the Lord for sending Jesus as the payment for my sin. My heart rejoices that the Father has allowed me to be a part of His family through faith in Christ.

It is important for us to pour out our concerns to our Father because He doesn't want us trying to carry our own burdens. His invitation is to

---

* See the back of this book for more information.

ask, seek, and knock. Sometimes I write down my requests for myself, my family, and others. I have a fantastic prayer journal that a friend of mine put together. It's called *On-Call Prayer* (because God is on call all the time—He never puts you on hold), and it is a wonderful way to journal through prayer.[3] Finally, I ask for His direction and leading throughout the day. It's interesting how thoughts pop into my head about things that need to be accomplished or issues I need to address or even how to order my day. I write down the thoughts He brings to mind as I ask Him to direct my path.

So that's how I come to the table with my Father. How about you? There's no perfect formula, just the invitation to dine with Him. Let us not neglect such an inviting feast with the King of all glory. Taste and see that the Lord is good.

Digging Deeper

Read Proverbs 3 and 4. In your journal, record all the benefits that come as a result of spending time with the Lord and trusting in Him.

DISCUSS

1. What blessing have you experienced personally from spending quiet time with the Lord?

2. What is your best time and place to meet with Him?

3. What are some of the distractions and things that may keep you from coming to the table to abide with the Lord?

HELPFUL RESOURCES

As I mentioned in the chapter, here are a few of my favorite devotionals. Most of them are available as e-books as well.

- *Streams in the Desert* by L.B.E. Cowman, updated by Jim Reimann
- *Spurgeon's Morning and Evening* by C.H. Spurgeon

- *The Seeking Heart* by François Fenelon
- *Thirty-One Days of Praise* by Ruth Myers
- *Praying the Names of God* by Ann Spangler
- *A Year with C.S. Lewis,* compiled by Patricia S. Klein
- *Each New Day* by Corrie ten Boom

Woman of the Word — Mrs. Farrar

Frederic William Farrar was born in Bombay (now called Mumbai) in 1831 and grew up to become a cleric of the Anglican Church, a school-teacher, and an author. His godly mother made such a strong impression on his life that you can't help but wonder if she was the reason he pursued a life of ministry. Here's what he wrote about her:

> My mother's habit was every day, immediately after break-fast, to withdraw for an hour to her own room, and to spend that hour in reading the Bible, in meditation and prayer. From that hour, as from a pure fountain, she drew the strength and sweetness which enabled her to fulfill all her duties and to remain unruffled by the worries and pet-tinesses which are so often the trial of narrow neighbor-hoods. As I think of her life, and all it had to bear, I see the absolute triumph of Christian grace in the lovely ideal of a Christian lady. I never saw her temper disturbed; I never heard her speak a word of anger, of calumny, or of idle gos-sip; I never observed in her any sign of a single sentiment unbecoming to a soul which had drank of the river of the water of life, and which had fed upon manna in the bar-ren wilderness. [4]

2

Daily Swim

As the deer pants for streams of water,
so my soul pants for you, my God.
My soul thirsts for God, for the living God.

PSALM 42:1-2

Bible reading is not an exceptional thing for the literate Christian.
It is a part of his response to God.

OSCAR FEUCHT

Recently I threw out a question on Facebook: "Why do you read the Bible? What's your motivation?" I must admit I was a bit surprised at the outpouring of enthusiastic responses. If you've ever thought the Bible had nothing to say to you personally, read a few of these comments.

- *Kay:* "I read it because I want to learn how to live the life that my Creator designed for me to live. I feel it is the owner's manual to learn what does work and what doesn't work to please our Father!"

- *Warren:* "Reading the Bible allows us to enter God's view of how life should and can be lived. Without the Bible we are trapped in the prevailing worldview of anger, selfishness, greed, hatred, lust, isolation, and other destructive attitudes and behaviors. But when we read the Bible, God breaks into our world with visions of His own, fostering community, forgiveness, love, faithfulness, and a host of other healthy attitudes."

Many talked about the Bible as their source for wisdom and guidance:

- *Penelope:* "God's Word brings me strength and wisdom to

face life's challenges on a daily basis. I know that I can trust the Bible to give me divine guidance because it is the inspired Word of God Himself."

- *Toddy*: "…To grow in my continued dependence on His wisdom and guidance and perspective in my life…to keep my eyes looking vertically to the things of eternal importance and not horizontally on my current circumstances."

Several agreed that the Bible helped them understand what God is like:

- *LaSharnda*: "My motivation is to learn more about the character of God so my character can be more like His. To learn about how I should live to impart that to others. To learn how to be more loving and to love others more sincerely."

- *Carrie*: "I want nothing more than to know Jesus more, and reading the Bible is my favorite way of finding and hearing Him. He has changed my whole life by the power of His Word. It truly is life to me."

I like Lisa's perspective:

- *Lisa*: "For me, it is my plumb line. For a builder building a home, everything is determined by the plumb line. It is the starting point; it is what you measure everything else against. It must all line up or the entire building will be off. This is what the Word of God is. Everything must be measured against it and in light of it."

With that kind of motivation, what is it that keeps us from reading His Word? Let's be honest, most of us realize the hearty benefits of knowing it, but when it actually comes down to reading it, we struggle to jump in. For some, it's fear of the unknown or not knowing where to start. Others complain, "I've tried to read the Bible, but I just don't understand it." It's surprising how many Christians have never read the entire Bible. In fact, many women I know attend Bible studies and prayer groups and read a myriad of devotionals, yet still haven't read the Bible all the way through. I want to encourage you that there is nothing more important than reading the Holy Scriptures for yourself and knowing what God has to say to you. Funny how we have time to read other things, but we don't make reading the very words of Almighty God a top priority.

Perhaps you've tried to read through the Bible. You started at the beginning in Genesis (and that was great—super-juicy stories) and then you began wading through Exodus, and by the time you got to Leviticus you decided to go thumb through a good magazine instead. Granted, there are some books that don't exactly make light reading. But don't let your past frustrations or your present intimidation keep you from jumping into the Word with both feet. Just as a swimmer must face her fear and take the first plunge, so we must be determined to dive right into the Bible with the Holy Spirit as our guide. My desire is to help you see how wonderful and powerful His Word is and to invite you to jump in and read it. Sure, it may take a moment or two for you to get acclimated to the water, but once you are in it, you will find great refreshment and joy for your life.

Maybe you are like me; I want to know what God has to say. I don't just want to sit on the side of the pool and let others tell me how great the water feels. I want to immerse myself in His truth. I want to know what He is like. I want to know about His power, His love, and His authority. I want to know how He intends to work through my life. The Bible gives me the answers. Reading it is different than studying it or meditating on it. Reading is an opportunity to get to know its content and follow its flow from beginning to end.

I like to think of *reading* the Bible as a vigorous morning swim through the Scriptures. Just as our physical bodies are strengthened through the exercise of swimming, so our faith is strengthened through the discipline of reading and getting to know God's Word. *Studying* the Bible is more like deep-sea treasure-diving, going deeper into His Word in order to discover great and rich truths we can apply to our lives. In chapter 3 we will look at a variety of methods for study, but in this chapter we will consider several ways to help you read through the Word with ease.

Finding a Plan That Is Right for You

My daughter Joy was a fitness director at a major corporation. Part of her job was to customize workout plans for her clients. No matter how perfect a personal fitness plan is for a client, it only works for that client if he or she will do it. Joy often said, "The most effective fitness program for you is the one you will actually do." Although running may help some people meet their fitness goals, if she prescribed a running program for someone who detests running or has bad knees, then it wouldn't be very effective. She had to find the program that worked best for the individual—one that made sense for them to actually carry out.

When you think about a plan, you need to consider your goal. Do you want to read the Bible through in a year? Perhaps you want to take two years to read the entire Bible. You may want to take each book slowly and read over the course of several years. You can also choose to read the books of the Bible as they were written chronologically, or you may want to read a little out of the Old and a little out of the New Testament each day. You can find a plan for just about any way you want to read the Bible.

As I mentioned earlier, the plan I use is the *One Year Bible*. You can buy this or *The Daily Bible*, which I also mentioned, at any bookstore or online store or you can get them as e-books. Again, the *One Year Bible* breaks the Scriptures down into dated daily readings of an Old Testament passage, a New Testament passage, a Psalm, and a Proverb. Some years I read through in a year, while other years I choose to read through the Old Testament in one year and the next year I read through the New Testament, along with Psalms and Proverbs. I have the *One Year Bible* on my iPad, so each morning I just open it up and read the portion for that day. *The Daily Bible* and the *One Year Chronological Bible* give you daily readings in the order that they were written. Also, most study Bibles include a plan to read the Bible through in a year.

Some Bible teachers suggest starting with the Gospel of John as a good introduction to who Jesus is and God's redemptive plan. Author and pastor R.C. Sproul offers a pattern for people who have never read the Bible. He suggests the following:

The Old Testament overview:

- Genesis (the history of creation, the fall, and God's covenantal dealings with the patriarchs)
- Exodus (the history of Israel's liberation and formation as a nation)

- Joshua (the history of the military conquest of the Promised Land)
- Judges (Israel's transition from a tribal federation to a monarchy)
- 1 Samuel (Israel's emerging monarchy under Saul and David)
- 2 Samuel (David's reign)
- 1 Kings (Solomon and the divided kingdom)
- 2 Kings (the fall of Israel)
- Ezra (the Israelites' return from exile)
- Nehemiah (the restoration of Jerusalem)
- Amos and Hosea (examples of minor prophets)
- Jeremiah (an example of a major prophet)
- Ecclesiastes (Wisdom Literature)
- Psalms and Proverbs (Hebrew poetry)

The New Testament overview:

- The Gospel of Luke (the life of Jesus)
- Acts (the early church)
- Ephesians (an introduction to the teaching of Paul)
- 1 Corinthians (life in the church)
- 1 Peter (an introduction to Peter)
- 1 Timothy (an introduction to the Pastoral Epistles)
- Hebrews (Christology)
- Romans (Paul's theology)

Sproul adds, "By reading these books, a student can get a basic feel for and understanding of the scope of the Bible without getting bogged down in the more difficult sections. From there, he or she can fill in the gaps to complete the reading of the entire Bible."[1]

Scripture Union is a ministry that offers tools to help both adults and children read, know, and love God's Word. They offer an Essential 100 Challenge (E100) as a way to read through the essential passages in Scripture. The E100 Challenge is based on 100 carefully selected short Bible passages, 50 from the Old Testament and 50 from the New. The plan helps you get the big picture of the Bible and also helps you keep up with your progress. They offer a little pocket-sized planner listing the Scriptures to read and providing a punch card so you can chart your progress. This is a great plan to do as a family or with other individuals. You can get the E100 planner at www.E100challenge.com.

Another tremendous resource for reading the Bible is www.Bible.com (the You Version), which offers a Bible app for your phone, iPod, tablet, or computer. You may already have their app, but did you know they offer reading plans as well? If you go to the "Plans" link on their menu, you will find a variety of ways to read the Bible. The cool thing is, the app keeps you informed on your progress and even gives you reminders if you are falling behind. You can choose a reading plan under the headings of Devotional, Topical, Partial Bible, Whole Bible, Youth, and Family. And You Version is constantly featuring new plans. The point is to find a plan that works for you. There are no perfect formulas for reading God's Word; the important thing is simply to do it.

We talked earlier about the value of finding a time and a place to get alone with God each day. I have found that when I have a time, a place, and a plan, I get the reading done. Without a plan, I aimlessly wander, picking a scripture here and scripture there and then eventually fizzle out. Make a plan. Choose it now. Whether it is to read one of the Psalms per day, or read the Gospel of John or read the Bible through in a year, start now. No excuses! Write down your plan for daily Bible reading on the line below:

My plan is to read: _____

_____

I will take _____ minutes every day to read His Word.

When I meet people who question the Bible, one of my first questions is, "Have you read it yourself?" Most of the apparent contradictions are pulled out of context and completely miss the intent of the passage. Reading the Bible pulls it all together and is a life-changing experience. As we get to know what it says and what it doesn't say, we come to recognize that it is the infallible Word of God. We can't read it too much. There's always something new to learn, a rich treasure to discover, or a great insight to uncover. Psalm 19:7 reminds us, "The statutes of the LORD are trustworthy, making wise the simple." In my life, reading the Bible has given me confidence and strength, insight and wisdom, patience and hope. More than anything else, it has given me Jesus.

Choosing a Translation

I'm embarrassed to tell you that I have five black skirts hanging in my closet. Five! Why in the world do I need five skirts, all the exact same color? That's the question my husband keeps asking me. I actually know exactly why I need each of those skirts. Although they are all black skirts, each fits me a little differently. Some are more casual, while others are for dressy occasions or business meetings. Let's not even talk about how many pairs of black shoes I have in my closet. You understand why I need all of them, don't you?

Perhaps you have asked similar questions about the different translations of the Bible. Why do we need so many types of Bibles and translations? How do you choose the right one for you? Is there one translation that is head and shoulders above the rest? Let me take you on a brief walk through the process of understanding the different translations in order for you to make an educated choice about the translation (or translations) that will work best for you. In section B, "All About Translations," in the "Good to Know" resources in the back of this book you will find a little more background as to how we got these translations as well as a helpful chart to assist you in making your decision.

Just as there are different fashion styles, different learning styles, and even different parenting styles, there are also different styles or philosophies when it comes to translating the Bible. Each has merit, yet each results in a somewhat different method of translation and how the resulting translation works for our personal use. Some translations are best used when studying and teaching the Bible, while others may be beneficial when simply reading or introducing it to someone who finds it difficult to understand. Let's consider the four different styles and make some sense of it all for ourselves. The four different styles are

- interlinear equivalence (word for word)
- formal equivalence (word for word)
- dynamic equivalence (thought for thought)
- paraphrase (which in the strictest sense is not really a translation, but we still need to know about it)

Allow me to break it down into bite-sized pieces.

Interlinear translation. An interlinear translation places an English word under every word in the original language. Whenever possible, one English word is directly under a word from the original text. These translations can make good study tools for Bible students, but tend to be awkward to use in teaching and reading. One key problem is that not all Hebrew or Greek words can be translated by a single English word. If you have ever studied a foreign language, you know that idioms and colloquialisms in a language often need to be paraphrased for a translation to make sense. Word order is also dramatically different from one language to the other. Also, some original words are grammatical markers and have no corresponding equivalent English words. *The Interlinear Bible* by Jay P. Green is an example of the interlinear translation approach.

Formal equivalence. Formal equivalence is a word-for-word translation as well, but it overcomes some of the challenges of the strict interlinear approach. For the most part, formal equivalence uses English that is clearer while remaining faithful to lexical details and grammatical structure of the original. There is less room for bias or misinterpretation with translations that seek to establish a formal equivalence between the original language and the English translation, yet they can still be awkward to read. Formal equivalence translations are good for Bible study and for teaching and preaching. The King James Version (KJV), New American Standard Bible (NASB), English Standard Version (ESV), Amplified Version, and Revised Standard Version (RSV) fall into the category of formal equivalence translations.

Dynamic equivalence. Dynamic equivalence (which has recently become known as "functional equivalence") is also termed *phrase-by-phrase* or *thought-for-thought* translation. It is concerned with accurately translating the *meaning* of the original rather than grammatical structure or matching the original word for word. It allows more room for interpretation, but is easier to understand. Examples of dynamic equivalence translations include the New Living Translation (NLT), the Good News Translation (GNT), and the Revised English Bible (REB). The dynamic equivalence is great for extensive reading and for more easily understanding the original meaning of the text.

Several translations attempt to strike a balance between thought-for-thought and word-for-word. Where they believe a word-for-word translation is not clear in English, they use a thought-for-thought translation. These include the New International Version (NIV), the Holman Christian Standard Bible (HCSB), and the New English Translation (NET). The benefit of these is that they try to employ the best of both philosophies.

Paraphrase. To paraphrase literally means to state something "beside" something else. In other words, it means to summarize a passage or text and put it in a person's or translator's own words. This is why a paraphrase is not a translation in the strictest sense, because it is not attempting to bring the exact words or thoughts of one language into another. It goes without saying that paraphrases are more vulnerable to bias, misinterpretation, and error. Basically you could say that a paraphrase is man's words about the Word of God. Two popular paraphrases are *The Living Bible* by Kenneth Taylor and *The Message* by Eugene Peterson.

Perhaps you are wondering which translation I prefer. I use quite a few different ones, and I use them at different times for different purposes. I read the New Living Translation for my daily quiet time (daily swim), and I use the New International Version and English Standard Version for more serious Bible study (deep-sea diving). I also like to use the King James and American Standard versions for cross-referencing passages to get a fuller picture of the meaning of a passage. Sometimes I refer

to the New English Translation (NET) Bible because it has the translators' notes.*

Which translation should you use? Allow me to offer a few thoughts.
First, I would suggest that you own several different translations—and
at least one study Bible (most translations offer a study Bible version)
because it will provide helpful notes, commentaries, and cross references
as well as maps, a dictionary, and a short concordance. Some even have
great articles in the back about different biblical topics. It is also helpful
to take note of the translation your church uses. You can be assured that
the pastors and staff at your church have carefully thought through which
translation they will use for preaching and to provide in the pews, so if you
agree with their doctrine you can lean on their research.

Make an educated decision using the information in this chapter and
in section B, "All About Translations," at the back of this book, as well as
from other sources. Visit a Christian bookstore and ask for a knowledge-
able staff person to assist you. Often Christian bookstores will have a chart
(much like the one at the end of this book) to help you think through the
comparisons. Most important, ask the Holy Spirit to lead you as you consider the right translation for you. Your biggest challenge is not choosing;
rather, it is avoiding the distractions that would keep you from reading it!
Let's be deliberate and determined to dive in and take a daily swim. The
water is perfect!

Digging Deeper

Read Psalm 19 and record in your journal all that you learn
about God's creation and the power of His Word.

DISCUSS

1. What are some of the reasons it is important to read the entire
   Bible?

---

* One more great resource I want to mention is called the *Life Essentials Study Bible* (Holman Bible
  Publishing), which uses the Holman Christian Standard Bible. It was put together by Dr. Gene Getz
  (over a seven-year period, no less!), and includes 1500 "Principles to Live By" developed by Gene,
  with expositions that are embedded right into the text using QR codes. It's fantastic, because as I
  am studying, I can stop and scan a QR code and listen to a message on the topic.

2. What is the difference between reading the Bible daily and studying it? Why do you need to do both?

3. What plan of action will you take to read God's Word daily?

HELPFUL RESOURCES

- *Living by the Book* by Howard and William Hendricks
- *Read the Bible for Life* by George H. Guthrie
- *The Story: The Bible as One Seamless Story from Beginning to End* (Zondervan)
- www.Bible.org
- *The Whole Bible Story: Everything That Happened in the Bible in Plain English* by William H. Marty

3

Diving Deeper

Study to show thyself approved unto God,
a workman that needeth not to be ashamed,
rightly dividing the word of truth.

2 Timothy 2:15 kjv

A thorough knowledge of the Bible
is worth more than a college education.

Theodore Roosevelt

Feeding a baby is an interesting process. If you've ever tried to coax a spoonful of rice cereal into the mouth of a stubborn eight-month-old, you know what I mean. "Here comes the airplane" and other lame attempts often get you nowhere. Thankfully, our precious little ones grow out of bottles and spoon-feedings. It is always a beautiful thing when our children learn to feed themselves. I loved it when my kids were able to begin putting Cheerios in their own mouth and stay occupied long enough for me to grab a few bites of my own lunch. The natural process of learning to feed oneself is a part of growing up and maturing. Wouldn't it be ridiculous to bottle-feed a teenager?

The writer of Hebrews uses this very metaphor when it comes to feeding ourselves the nourishing food of God's Word. The writer admonishes believers to grow up and feed themselves. Here's the challenge from Hebrews:

> Though by this time you ought to be teachers, you need
> someone to teach you the elementary truths of God's word
> all over again. You need milk, not solid food! Anyone who
> lives on milk, being still an infant, is not acquainted with
> the teaching about righteousness. But solid food is for the

mature, who by constant use have trained themselves to distinguish good from evil (Hebrews 5:12-14).

Certainly, there is a place to be spiritually fed by others (at church, listening to podcasts, in small groups and Bible studies), but we also need to learn to feed ourselves and be able to discern and distinguish between good and evil, truth and untruth. I want to grow up, don't you? Ultimately we want to be mature in our faith and study God's Word on our own, so that we can rightly discern it. We don't want to take what a teacher has to say for granted. Luke (the writer of Acts) pointed out that the believers in Berea were of "more noble character" because they received the message of the gospel with great eagerness and examined the Scriptures every day to see if what Paul said was true (Acts 17:11). We too can be like the Bereans, searching the Scriptures in order to discern what is true.

Comedian George Carlin observed, "I was thinking about how people seem to read the Bible a whole lot more as they get older. Then it dawned on me—they're cramming for their final exam." The truth is, we are not simply studying for our final exam, we are studying to know more about who God is and how He wants us to live. We want to know the very words of our Creator! The apostle Paul wrote, "All Scripture is God-breathed and is useful for teaching, rebuking, correcting and training in righteousness, so that the servant of God may be thoroughly equipped for every good work" (2 Timothy 3:16-17). That's a great list of benefits!

Notice Paul used the word *equipped*. If I were going on a camping trip, I'd want to be equipped with the right gear and tools for survival. In a similar way, we want to be equipped for life. If the words we have in the Bible are God-breathed and useful to our lives, then we certainly want to study them to know what they have to say to us personally. The Bible teaches us. It rebukes us, and helps us recognize sin in our lives. It corrects us, like a ship whose path is corrected by the captain when it is veering off course. It trains us so we know how to live righteous lives. God has given us His Word to equip us in order to do the good work He has placed us on this earth to do.

In this chapter, I will give you some tools and techniques to help you dig deeper as you study on your own. I know there are great Bible studies you can attend or books you can use at home, but I also hope that you will be able to do your own exploration. It's the difference between letting someone else spoon-feed you and feeding yourself. If we want God's Word to become personal in our lives—if we want to truly fall in love with it—we need to explore it on our own. Ultimately, when it comes to studying for a class in school, we can't expect someone else to study for us.

Book by Book

As I mentioned in the previous chapter, a good study Bible is a useful tool for any Bible student. I also encourage you to have a notebook or journal to use specifically for your personal study. The study Bibles I use are the New International Version *Life Application Study Bible* (Tyndale House Publishers), the *English Standard Version Study Bible* (Crossway Publishers), and the *HCSB Life Essentials Bible* (Holman Publishers). Each of these Bibles offers extensive study notes, commentaries, and cross references, passage by passage. They also introduce each book of the Bible describing the time period of when it was written and the context in which it was written. Plus they offer an overview of each book as well as maps, charts, and other helpful references.

Once you have found a study Bible that is right for you, it's time to take your first steps forward. One method of study is book by book, taking one book of the Bible at a time and digging deep to get to know it and discover how it applies to your life. I want us to walk through a passage together so we can get a feel for how to do a personal, inductive Bible study. Our steps will include *pray, read, observe, consider,* and *apply.* Let's look at the book of Ruth as we walk through these steps together.

Pray. The psalmist wrote a simple prayer: "Open my eyes, that I may behold wonderful things from thy law" (Psalm 119:18 KJV). As we begin our study, let's ask God to open our eyes to see His truths and our hearts to understand how He wants to apply it to our lives. I'm thankful for His Spirit who leads us to understanding and guides us all along the way.

Read. Read through the entire book of Ruth. At this point you are simply reading, not studying, in order to get a general overview of the book. After reading the book through, make a few notes in your journal. Record the general theme, who the author is, and what the context is for the writing.

Your study Bible will help you with some of this information. As you read, it is important to note what type of literature you are reading. Is it historical, poetic, or prophetic? Knowing the type of literature you are looking at will assist you as you make observations and consider how to apply the passage. For instance, if the passage you are reading is prophetic and is meant for a certain time and a certain people, then we must be cautious of taking those words and applying them to our own situation.

Observe. Observation means opening our eyes to what a passage is saying. We must ask questions such as *who, what, why, where, when,* and *how.* Each book of the Bible is broken down into chapters and verses, and most study Bibles will break chapters down into sections. This makes it easier to study passage by passage through a book. For instance, in the book of Ruth, the first chapter can be broken down into two sections: 1:1-5 and 1:6-22. Here's the first section:

Naomi Loses Her Husband and Sons

> In the days when the judges ruled, there was a famine in the land. So a man from Bethlehem in Judah, together with his wife and two sons, went to live for a while in the country of Moab. The man's name was Elimelek, his wife's name was Naomi, and the names of his two sons were Mahlon and Kilion. They were Ephrathites from Bethlehem, Judah. And they went to Moab and lived there.
>
> Now Elimelek, Naomi's husband, died, and she was left with her two sons. They married Moabite women, one named Orpah and the other Ruth. After they had lived there about ten years, both Mahlon and Kilion also died, and Naomi was left without her two sons and her husband.

Now let's apply our observation skills to this passage. In your notebook, write down the six questions (*who, what, where, why, when,* and *how*) on the left-hand side of your page, leaving spaces between each question. Answer each of the questions about this passage from Ruth.

Who? We find quite a few names mentioned here in these few verses.

You should have written down Elimelek, Naomi, Mahlon, Kilion, Orpah, and Ruth. Also we see groups of people mentioned, the Ephrathites and the Moabites. As I mentioned earlier, whenever you are starting to study a new book, it is also important to ask, Who wrote this book and to whom is he writing?

What? What happens in this passage? Again, in this short passage we learn quite a bit: there was famine in the land, a man of Bethlehem took his wife and sons to live in Moabite country. Elimelek dies, leaving Naomi a widow with her two sons. Her sons marry Moabite women, but then her sons die. Naomi has lost her husband and two sons. Another "What" question that may come to mind is, "What did God's law say about marrying foreign wives?" Here we would need to look at other references in the Bible, which may be in the margin of your study Bible. Relations with the Moabites were discouraged but most likely not forbidden, as you will find in Deuteronomy 23:3-6.

Where? The two locations mentioned are Bethlehem and Moab. Moab was the land east of the Dead Sea. In your study Bible you will probably find a map. Take a look at the map and locate both the city of Bethlehem and the Moabite land.

Why? To the obvious question of why Elimelek went to Moab, the simple answer would be, *Because there was a famine.* But if we dig deeper and think about additional "why" questions, there are some left unanswered. Why did Elimelek choose to go to the despised country of the Moabites instead of staying in Bethlehem like most of the Israelites? Why did the sons marry Moabite wives? Why did they all die so early? What additional questions come to your mind?

When? From our study Bible we can find out that the book of Ruth was written around 1100 BC, while Israel was dwelling in the land God had provided for them, the Promised Land. It was a time when the judges ruled the people and Israel had already gone through periods of rebellion, punishment, and repentance. We also know it was during a time of famine in the land.

How? Perhaps the most important *how* question we can ask in any passage is "How do we see God at work?" We can also ask questions like, "How did Elimelek respond to the famine? Did he trust God?" "How did God use the famine as a part of His overall plan?"

Additionally, as we observe the passage we should look for words or themes that are repeated. Sadly, death seems to be the recurring theme in this passage. What else do you notice?

Consider. Once we have made observations and asked questions, then it is time to consider what we can learn from the passage. One of the main questions we must consider every time we read or study a section is, "What do I learn about God?" We must also ask, "What is God teaching His people through this passage?" Again, as you consider the message He is relaying through His Word, keep in mind the type of literature you are reading and the context in which it was given. We know that Ruth is a historical book that is relaying a story of a Hebrew family during the time of the judges. Although it reveals the heritage of David, who would later become king, it also gives us a picture of redemption and teaches us numerous life lessons. Knowing the big picture of the book of Ruth, reread the short passage we looked at earlier (Ruth 1:1-5). What lessons seem to surface from these initial few verses?

First, God in His sovereignty allowed a famine in the nation of Israel. Sometimes in Scripture we see that famines were a providential punishment for disobedience. In Deuteronomy 11:13-14 God reminded the Israelites, "If you faithfully obey the commands I am giving you today—to love the LORD your God and to serve him with all your heart and with all your soul—then I will send rain on your land in its season, both autumn and spring rains, so that you may gather in your grain, new wine and olive oil."

Sometimes God used famines to advance His purposes, as in the case of Joseph and his brothers in Egypt. Initially Elimelek's plan to move to Moabite territory didn't turn out to be such a great idea, yet God had a bigger plan. In the big scheme, God's plan was to bring Ruth and Boaz together; eventually the Messiah would be born through their lineage. God can take what seems like a challenge or a tragedy or even a mistake and use it for a bigger, better, and more eternal purpose. What a great lesson to consider! Ultimately, God can take our misfortunes and use them for a greater purpose. Although the book starts with tragedy, it ends with delight.

Another lesson to consider as we look at this passage is, How do we respond to challenges? When the famine came, Elimelek packed up and left to go to Moab, which was traditionally Israel's enemy. Were there others who did the same thing? Should Elimelek have stayed and prayed for God's help instead? Pause for a moment to consider how you handle difficulties. Do you run to the easiest solution, or do you stop and pray and seek God's guidance? We are not told in this passage whether Elimelek sought the Lord before going to Moab, so we don't know, but all I can think of is Psalm 34 where David wrote, "I sought the LORD, and he answered me; he delivered me from all my fears. Those who look to Him are radiant; their faces are never covered in shame." What a powerful reminder to seek the Lord before making a move.

Bad starts don't always mean a bad story. In fact, sad happenings can lead to great victories in the end. The cross of Christ is a perfect example. What seemed like the world's greatest tragedy to the disciples turned out to be the world's greatest victory—redemption. In the book of Ruth we also see a beautiful picture of tragedy leading to redemption. What are some other lessons that God is teaching you through the first few verses in Ruth? Prayerfully consider the lessons God wants you to learn from this passage. Reflect on some of the other Bible passages that are referenced in the margin of your study Bible. Think about what God is teaching you about Himself. What is He teaching you about His power and authority? What do you learn about sin, disobedience, and responsibility? Record your thoughts in your journal.

Apply. After we have read, observed, and considered the passage we are reading, we don't want to walk away from it without applying it to our lives personally. This is where we ask the question, "As a result of studying this passage, how should I live?" What thoughts initially come to your mind?

_____

_____

_____

I am challenged by this passage to seek God's direction in every area of my life. One way I can practically apply what I learned is to spend time in prayer each day, seeking God's direction as I plan my day and looking to Him for guidance throughout the day.

Word Study

There may be times when you are curious about a certain word or phrase in the Bible and want to do a specific study on it. Not too long ago I was asked to speak to a group of women on the specific topic "Reflecting God's Glory." I wasn't exactly sure where to start with this message, so I decided to do a word study on the word *glory* in the Bible. I bought a notebook and began to explore the word as it is used throughout Scripture.

My first resource was *Strong's Exhaustive Concordance*, a huge book with just about every word in the Bible listed alphabetically, showing the references where the word is found in both the Old Testament and the New Testament. In my opinion, this is an essential reference book if you are planning to do a thorough word study. Strong's concordance was compiled in 1890 and is still a tremendous tool for Bible students today. The best part about this concordance is that each word has a number beside it (called a Strong's Number) that correlates to the original word in Greek or Hebrew based on the King James Version of the Bible.

When you look up a word, you will first see the word in bold followed by a number in parenthesis. This number tells you how many times the word is found in the Bible. Next you will find a list of the phrases using the word along with the references (where it is found) in the Bible. After each reference you will see the Strong number. If the number is in bold print, it is referring to a Hebrew word, and if it is in italics it refers to the Greek. The next step is to look up the numbers in Strong's dictionary, which is located in the back of the concordance.

When I did the *glory* word study, I found 402 references to the word in the Bible. Oh my! I also found that there were several different Greek and Hebrew words that were translated into the word *glory*. I decided to do my word study by looking up each verse in the Bible with the word *glory* and writing down the verse in my journal. Phew! That was quite an exhaustive word study! I also wrote down which Hebrew or Greek word it was referring to in context. I did this study bit by bit for several weeks and came to a fuller understanding of God's glory and what it means to reflect it. You may not need to look up every single reference when you do a word study, but you do want to look up a variety of ways the word is used and consider not only its context but also its application for your life.

It is important to remember that context is key in understanding a word or phrase. Be sure to look at the passages as a whole to understand who is speaking and who they are speaking to. As far as getting a Strong's concordance, I happened to get mine from a friend who was giving away a few books from his library. You can order the book online from Christian Book Distributors (www.cbd.com). Or consider visiting a half-price bookstore. Since this is a long-available reference book, the content hasn't changed since 1890. It is a big book, so it helps to find it at a discount (Most study Bibles have a condensed concordance at the back of the book.)

For a more comprehensive explanation of Hebrew or Greek words, you may want to use a Hebrew or Greek lexicon. A free online reference is www.BlueLetterBible.org, which offers amazingly helpful word study tools. Just go to their website and type in a word and you can click on dictionaries, biblical references, Greek and Hebrew lexicons, interlinear Bible, and additional commentaries and devotionals. Another tremendous resource is Logos Bible Software (www.Logos.com), which provides a gigantic library of resources and commentaries. The thing I like most about it is you can even listen to sermons on a topic or a passage.

As you embark on studying God's Word for yourself, you will find a rich treasure awaiting you. My hope is that as you study, you will develop a deeper connection with the God who loves you and wants you to know His heart of love. Every time you dig into the Scriptures you will discover new and wonderful truths about God and the depths of His love for you. He invites us to dig into the vast treasure of His resources, for there are always magnificent discoveries waiting to be found. What riches we behold when we dive deep into the ocean of His Word! "Oh, the depth of the riches of the wisdom and knowledge of God! How unsearchable his judgments, and his paths beyond tracing out!" (Romans 11:33).

Digging Deeper

Read the next section of Ruth (Ruth 1:6-22) and continue the inductive study of this amazing book, recording your observations and application in your journal.

DISCUSS

1. Why is it important for all believers to learn how to study the Bible for themselves?

2. What is your personal motivation for studying God's Word?

3. Have you set a time and place where you will study the Bible on a regular basis?

HELPFUL RESOURCES

- *Basic Bible Interpretation* by Roy B. Zuck
- *How to Study Your Bible* by Kay Arthur
- *How to Study the Bible* by R.A. Torrey

Woman of the Word

Corrie ten Boom risked her life for the sake of God's Word. Corrie was born in Haarlem, the Netherlands, in 1892; her father was a watchmaker and a committed Christian who built his life on biblical principles. When the Nazi persecution of the Jews began, Corrie's family hid Jewish people in a special hiding place between the walls of their home. Her father taught his family that these were the people through whom God chose to bring the Holy Scriptures and the Messiah, and that is why he felt that his family must do their part to protect them. When the Nazis eventually figured out that the family was hiding Jews, Corrie and her family were imprisoned.

Corrie and her sister, Betsie, spent ten months in three different prisons, the last being the infamous Ravensbrück concentration camp located near Berlin, Germany. As they were entering Ravensbrück, Corrie and Betsie were lined up with the other prisoners to be processed. Corrie prayed for God's direction and protection for her precious Bible. God somehow led her to a wooden bench in a deserted toilet and shower room. Although the bench was covered with roaches, it gave her a hiding place for her Bible, which she had been hiding in a pouch strung round her neck.

She was able to keep her Bible, and it became her and Betsie's sustenance, despite the horrible conditions. Although life in the camp seemed unbearable at times, Corrie and Betsie used their time there to share the comforting truths and rich treasures of the Scripture with their fellow prisoners. Many women became Christians as a result. Sadly, Betsie died in Ravensbrück, yet Corrie survived and went on to travel the world, sharing the love of Christ and the power of His Word.

In a devotional written years after her time in the prison camps, she wrote,

> Unhappiness in the Christian life is very often due to our failure to realize the greatness of the Gospel. The Gospel is not something partial. It takes in the whole life, the whole of history, the whole world. It tells about the Creation and the final judgment and everything in between. It is a complete whole view of life. It covers every eventuality in our experience. The Gospel is meant to control and govern everything in our lives. We must dwell more on our riches. *Let the word of Christ dwell in you richly—Colossians 3:16* KJV.[1]

4

Breathe It In

May these words of my mouth and this meditation of my heart
be pleasing in your sight,
Lord, my Rock and my Redeemer.

Psalm 19:14

Lay hold on the Bible until the Bible lays hold on you.

Will H. Houghton

What comes to mind when you hear the word *meditate*? When I was a child growing up in the 1960s (don't start counting to figure out how old I am) the term *meditate* was reserved for hippies or people caught up in Eastern mysticism. As Christians, we steered clear of the word because *those* groups seemed to have a monopoly on it. Thankfully, the term has been re-introduced to the Christian culture—although we should have never been afraid of a word that is used throughout Scripture, which repeatedly encourages us to meditate on God's Word. Once we get to know what meditation means in its truest sense, we will see how essential meditating on God's Word is in our daily lives.

The Hebrew word most commonly translated *meditate* is *hagah*, which, surprisingly, means "to moan or growl." It is pronounced "haw-gaw" (emphasis on the second syllable) and is thought to be an onomatopoetic term reflecting the sighing and low sounds a person makes while musing or pondering. Personally, I don't typically moan or make "haw-gaw" sounds when I am in the depths of contemplating something, but I guess the ancients did.

The implication of *hagah* is that the reader is so moved by what they are taking in that they erupt into audible moaning. Does God's Word move you to that extent? When you reflect and ponder the Scriptures, are you so taken by its wisdom, conviction, and authority that sighing is the natural release? That's some serious *hagah*, my friends! I want the Word to move me and change me, but I must admit all too often I read it in a hurry without allowing it to affect me at all. Yet God desires us to meditate on His Word continually. In the book of Joshua, we find that God instructed the Israelite leader to meditate (*hagah*). Here's what He said to Joshua: "Keep this Book of the Law always on your lips; meditate on it day and night, so that you may be careful to do everything written in it. Then you will be prosperous and successful" (Joshua 1:8).

In Psalm 1 *hagah* is used again, with a similar charge and promise:

> Blessed is the one
>   who does not walk in step with the wicked
> or stand in the way that sinners take
>   or sit in the company of mockers,
> but whose delight is in the law of the LORD,
>   and who *meditates* on his law day and night.
> That person is like a tree planted by streams of water,
>   which yields its fruit in season
> and whose leaf does not wither—
>   whatever they do prospers
> (Psalm 1:1-3).

I want to love God's Word so much that it shakes my very being and causes me to obey it. As I ponder it, I don't want to simply read it and walk away and forget what I have read. I want to get my very nourishment and growth from it. Meditating on the Word is meant to move us deeply and internally so that it not only makes us moan or sigh or haw-*gaw*, but also pushes us into action and into obedience. His Word is not to be taken lightly—we are to feel it and experience it deeply. One of the benefits of meditating on it continually is that it produces a fruitful, prosperous life.

How is meditating on God's Word different than reading it or studying it? When we read it, we are getting to know the content, and when we study His Word, we are digging deeper in research and exploration. Both reading and studying engage the mind in processing the words of the Bible, yet meditation involves not only the mind, but also the depths of the heart. It is experiencing His Word mentally and emotionally, contemplating it so that it moves us into action. It means looking intently at a portion of Scripture and letting it affect our lives. Dr. Jim Denison often says, "Every time you read the Bible you should be different when you are done. If you are not different, then you are not done."

A Mirror

Have you ever checked the mirror just after you finished a great meal and noticed that you had a piece of lettuce or something green stuck in your teeth? Then you start trying to think of all the people who saw you, and you are also miffed at the people (your so-called friends) who didn't tell you about the stuff in your teeth. Right? Been there? Can you imagine going to the mirror, seeing the green stuff in your teeth, and then just walking away and doing nothing about it? Never! That's crazy. Yet, that's how the apostle James describes the person who reads God's Word and doesn't allow it to change them or make a difference in their lives. They read it, but don't put it into practice. Smiling with lettuce in their teeth! Yuck!

Here's how he put it:

> Do not merely listen to the word, and so deceive yourselves. Do what it says. Anyone who listens to the word but does not do what it says is like someone who looks at his face in a mirror and, after looking at himself, goes away and immediately forgets what he looks like. But whoever looks intently into the perfect law that gives freedom, and continues in it—not forgetting what they have heard, but doing it—they will be blessed in what they do (James 1:22-25).

Pope Gregory I expressed it this way: "The Holy Bible is like a mirror before our mind's eye. In it we see our inner face. From the Scriptures we can learn our spiritual deformities and beauties." Notice the last sentence of the passage from James, "Whoever looks intently into the perfect law…and continues in it…they will be blessed in what they do." There's that mention of a blessing again! It is for those who look intently into His Word and live it out. We don't want to just look or read the Word smugly and then go and do our own thing. The Bible is a life-changer! It is a reflector! It should make a difference in our lives. James encourages us to not simply glance at the Word, but to look at it intently and do what it says.

The word *look* used by James is the Greek word *parakupto*, which refers to stooping down in order to get a good look at something. In other words, this means we are in serious observation here. We are not just running by and grabbing a quick glance as we rush through our day. We must pause a moment if we are to stoop and observe something. In a similar way, may we be as intent in our observation of God's Word and what it is saying to us personally. Let's not just rush through reading a daily Bible passage so we can check it off our list as done. May our prayer be, *Lord, help me to see what You want me to see in Your Word. Help me to look intentionally and learn from it. Don't let me walk away and not allow Your Word to change me. Give me strength to obey and continue in it, walking in it, strengthened by it, convicted from it, inspired because of it.*

Being blessed and fruitful is a natural result of meditating on His Word. Why? Because as we meditate on it, we come to know the heart of God. We are moved and motivated to walk in obedience. When we are immersed in His Word, we also live with a perspective of hope in what He can do, rather than living in despair of our circumstances. We are also continually aware of His love and His presence in our lives. To be blessed literally means to be happy. Certainly a person who is deeply moved by the truths of the Bible and experiences God's loving presence in their lives is a happy, blessed person.

How to Effectively Meditate on the Scriptures

Meditation is where God's Word meets our hearts. Perhaps the reason so few people meditate on it is because it means we must slow down and be attentive. Let's admit it, our society today is going in the opposite direction. Most of us would describe our lives as busy and distracted, with a huge deficit of still time and attention to people and God's Word. So how do we do it? What does it look like in a practical sense to meditate on the Scriptures?

Meditation is a continual action; it's a bit like breathing. Breathing out our cares and selfish concerns and breathing in the truth of His Word. In both the Joshua and the Psalms passages, we see the implication of meditating day and night. Even the passage from James speaks of the continual action of looking intently into His Word. Think about it this way: when we go for a swim, we are actively swimming and breathing. But when we stop swimming, we are still breathing (hopefully), and we continue to breathe day and night. As we read and contemplate passages from the Bible during our daily swim, we can meditate on the passage by continuing to think and ponder it throughout our day.

Let's experience what I'm talking about right now. Stop for a moment and be still. Breathe out the cares and worries you are probably carrying around in your mind and heart right now. Give them over to the Lord in prayer and thank Him for His care and His presence. Now let's breathe in a truth from His Word. Thoughtfully read the following passage several times. You may even want to say it aloud if you are by yourself.

> I have loved you with an everlasting love;
> I have drawn you with loving-kindness
> (Jeremiah 31:3).

Think about each word. Ask the Holy Spirit to teach you and speak into your heart. Ask Him to show you something fresh and new from this passage. Write down the thoughts that come to you on the lines below.

_____

_____

_____

What simple truth can you take with you throughout your day today?

_____

_____

_____

How does this truth change you personally?

_____

_____

_____

Simply put, meditation is being attentive to what the Scripture is saying and breathing it into your daily life. I encourage you to consider and ponder on a thought or phrase from your daily swim (your daily Bible reading). You may want to write a verse or phrase on an index card and carry it with you during the day. The thing that sets Christian meditation apart from all the other types of meditation is that our meditation is centered on God's truth, the Bible. As we take time to be still and ponder, our meditation is directed toward God's written Word, not some nebulous thought out there that we grab and repeat, as in Eastern mysticism. In each of our passages (Joshua 1:8, Psalm 1, and James 1:25), meditation is characterized by intensity, continual motion (day and night), and a focus on His Word.

Shaken and Stirred

Meditation should not only stir our hearts with the powerful truths and wisdom of the Bible, but it must also shake us up and move us to action. God told Joshua to meditate on the Law day and night so he would "do everything written in it." Similarly, James wrote that we are to not merely listen to the Word, but do what it says. As we contemplate the Word, it should stir us to obedience. The Latin word for *obedience* is *obaudire*, which actually means to listen with great attentiveness. Do you see how taking in God's Word and obedience are completely linked together? He wants us to listen and to walk with Him.

Dietrich Bonhoeffer, imprisoned during World War II for subversive activity against Hitler's regime, wrote, "Daily, quiet reflection on the Word of God as it applies to me becomes for me a point of crystallization for everything that gives interior and exterior order to my life." He continued, "Why do I meditate? Because I am a Christian. Therefore, every day in which I do not penetrate more deeply into the knowledge of God's Word in Holy Scripture is a lost day for me." [2]

As we meditate, let us turn to His Spirit within us, seeking His leadership and guidance throughout our day. He will enable us to live according to God's Word. Paul put it this way, "My dear friends, as you have always obeyed—not only in my presence, but now much more in my absence—continue to work out your salvation with fear and trembling, for it is God who works in you to will and to act in order to fulfill his good purpose" (Philippians 2:12-13). The term *working out our salvation* means living it out daily. It is God's Spirit who is working in us both to will and to act according to His good purpose. As we turn to the Spirit, who dwells within us, through contemplation and prayer, He moves us to walk in obedience and experience fruitfulness in our lives.

Father, draw us to Your Word in a deeper, richer way. Let us not only learn it in our minds, but experience it in our hearts and live it out in our lives. May we live in constant communion with You and Your truth. Stir in our hearts the greatest truth of all, the fact that You love us with an unfailing love. Let us walk in Your love all day long.

Oh, how I love your law! I meditate on it all day long.

PSALM 119:97

Digging Deeper

Read Psalm 23. Take one verse or phrase at a time and contemplate it and meditate on it throughout your day. In your journal, record what God is teaching you.

DISCUSS

1. Why do you think meditating on God's Word is important to living the Christian life?

2. How is meditating on His Word different from reading it or studying it?

3. How do meditation and obedience go together?

HELPFUL RESOURCES

- *Reflection on the Word Devotional* by Ken Gire
- *Meditating on the Word* by Dietrich Bonhoeffer
- *The Joy of my Heart, Meditating Daily on God's Word* by Anne Graham Lotz

Woman of the Word

Although Simone Weil lived on this earth for only 33 years, her writings continue to bless countless men and women today. When Simone was in her late twenties she visited a Trappist abbey and there wrote that "Christ took hold of" her. It was from that time forward that she grew deeper in her love for Jesus and His divine nature, and was forever changed by the meaning of the Passion. Simone was educated in philosophy and was an experienced schoolteacher. She was also a prolific writer, focusing on prayer and the contemplative experience. She died in 1943 while serving with French Resistance forces in England and trying to survive on the food rations of a French workman in occupied France. After World War II her insights on prayer made her "a kind of apostle of the spiritual life in France."[1]

One of her best-known works is entitled *Waiting for God* (eventually published by Harper & Row in 1973). In this book she meditated on the Lord's Prayer and took each phrase bit by bit, contemplating and pondering its meaning. Here is a brief excerpt of her meditation on the phrase "Thy will be done."

> We have to desire that everything that has happened should have happened, and nothing else. We have to do so, not because what has happened is good in our eyes, but because God has permitted it, and because the obedience of the course of events to God is in itself an absolute good.

5

Never Go Anywhere
Without It

Keep my commands and you will live;
guard my teachings as the apple of your eye.
Bind them on your fingers;
write them on the tablet of your heart.

PROVERBS 7:2-3

We must study the Bible more.
We must not only lay it up within us,
but transfuse it through the whole texture of the soul.

HORATIUS BONAR

*S*everal weeks ago my friend Becky enthusiastically shared with me her most recent housecleaning discovery—a microfiber cloth. This isn't just any microfiber cloth; it is a super-mega-absorbent one that cleans like magic. Becky demonstrated its cleaning power by taking a stick of butter and rubbing it on her sliding glass doors. Then she just took her wet "Wonder Cloth" and wiped down the glass. It was amazingly clean, without a streak! She went on to show me how she could get red stains out of carpet and wipe up yucky spills on the countertop—all using only water and the cloth, no chemicals! This little cloth looked like any other cloth, but it had an amazing hidden power. I can see why she was so excited to find this little gem. It almost makes housecleaning fun (almost).

What if I shared with you something that had supermiraculous cleansing power, not for your house but for your life? Just as Becky's cloth removes even the toughest stains, so the Bible has the ability to clean us up. Paul wrote this to the Ephesians:

> Husbands, love your wives, just as Christ loved the church
> and gave himself up for her to make her holy, cleansing
> her by the washing with water through the word, and to
> present her to himself as a radiant church, without stain
> or wrinkle or any other blemish, but holy and blameless
> (Ephesians 5:25-27).

Isn't that beautiful? Yes, I know the part about husbands loving their wives is beautiful, but also the part that says we are cleansed by the "washing with water through the word." The Holy Spirit (symbolized by water here) uses the Word to purify our lives.

I'm reminded of what James wrote: "Get rid of all moral filth and the evil that is so prevalent and humbly accept the word planted in you, which can save you" (James 1:21). James refers to the Word planted in us. It is difficult for the Word to cleanse us if we don't know His Word, but if it is planted in us, it can keep us from getting in a whole lot of trouble. The psalmist wrote, "Thy Word have I hid in mine heart, that I might not sin against Thee" (Psalm 119:11 KJV). Further, John wrote to the early believers, "I write to you young men, because you are strong and the word of God lives in you, and you have overcome the evil one" (1 John 2:14). In each of these passages we see the power of the Word of God as it lives, dwells, and is hidden in us.

The Bible is living and powerful, sharper than any two-edged sword, so why wouldn't we want to carry it in our minds and hearts wherever we go? It's funny, but we wouldn't be caught dead without our cell phones, right? How much more important is it for us to carry the Word of God with us everywhere we go? Perhaps you are thinking, *If I have my smart phone with me, then I can just look up the scripture I want to find using my Scripture app.* In some ways that seems to make sense, but the difference is that when God's Word is dwelling in your mind it is always ready to be applied, whether it is to comfort a friend or to convict us of sin or to help us discern which direction to go. It's like the difference between knowing a song by heart and having to look up the words every time you want to sing it.

The challenge is that memorizing a song seems easy, but memorizing Scripture often seems like an impossible mountain to climb. Although it is an old urban myth that we only use 10 percent of our brain capacity, it is also a myth that you can't teach old dogs new tricks. We can continually learn and grow and stretch our intellectual capabilities, and sometimes it just takes a new strategy. Just like Becky's super-absorbent cloth, our brains have a vast ability to absorb information. If you have tried to memorize Scripture before and feel like an utter failure, never fear! There are a variety of ways to learn and memorize—you just need to find the strategy that works best for you. I employ quite a few different methods to help me hold onto Scripture. By the end of this chapter, I hope to have helped you memorize at least one verse of Scripture, and I also hope I can motivate you to memorize many more!

I personally find it inspiring to read about others who have proven the ability to memorize large amounts of Scripture. Perhaps one of the lives that motivates me the most is that of Frances Ridley Havergal. Born in Worcestershire, England, in 1836, Frances was to Great Britain what Fanny Crosby was to the United States. Undoubtedly you are familiar with some of her beloved hymns: "Take My Life and Let It Be" and "Like a River Glorious." She was a prolific hymn writer and poet, as well as an accomplished musician. Although she faced many challenges in her life, both physically and circumstantially, her faith remained strong and her foundation was in God's Word. Her daily quiet time with the Lord was kept with a devoted discipline, but what is most fascinating about this woman was her commitment to Bible memory.

After she passed away in 1879, her sisters revealed that she had memorized all of the Gospels and epistles, as well as Isaiah (her favorite book), the Psalms, the Minor Prophets, and Revelation![1] I can't help but think that her deep passion for God was a result of the Scripture she hid within her heart. One biographer described Frances in this way: "Simply and sweetly she sang the love of God, and His way of salvation. To this end, and for this object, her whole life and all her powers were consecrated. She lives and speaks in every line of her poetry. Her poems are permeated with the fragrance of her passionate love of Jesus."[2]

Can you believe all that Frances held in her head? Through her example I became convinced I could memorize a little more than I thought I could. So when our Sunday-school teacher at church challenged all of us in the class to memorize the third chapter of Colossians, I took on the challenge and did it! Now I want you to know that I am not some intellectual. I'm just a normal person with a determination to carry God's Word with me wherever I go.

After I had memorized Colossians 3, a family friend told me he was trying to memorize large portions of Scripture as well, so we challenged each other to memorize one chapter per month. At the end of each month we would meet together along with our spouses and recite our passages. At first, I embarked on memorizing the fourth chapter of Philippians (mainly because I was familiar with most of the verses in the chapter), but after I memorized Philippians 4, it made sense to conquer the first three chapters as well. After four months, I completed memorizing the entire book of Philippians. Colossians came next and then 1 John.

I'm telling you this not to say, *Look at me*. I'm telling you this because I want you to know that if an ordinary girl like me can memorize entire chapters and books of the Bible, it's possible for you too. I want to share my memorization tips and secrets with you so you can join me in becoming a memorizing machine! The most important ingredient you need is the desire to do it. Memorizing Scripture has deepened my own understanding of God's love for me. Not only does memorizing His Word strengthen my own spiritual journey, but it also allows me to share God's Word with a friend or associate or neighbor whenever the need arises. As a Bible teacher, my messages are more powerful as I interject Scripture from my heart. One other benefit is that the more I memorize, the easier it gets. I'm keeping my mind young and fresh and growing. Some people do puzzles and mind exercises to keep their brains alert, but what could be more meaningful and life-giving than memorizing Scripture?

When it comes to God's Word, I don't want to be an undernourished pauper. I want to be rich and full, with His Word dwelling in me and overflowing from me. How about you? Paul wrote to the Colossians, "Let the word of God dwell in you richly as you teach and admonish one another with all wisdom." The opposite of letting the Word dwell in you richly is to let it dwell in you poorly. I want to be rich and overflowing with the truth of God's Word, and I'm sure you do too.

Picture It

When I was in high school, my dad purchased two tickets to a Scripture memory seminar, and since my mom couldn't go, he took me. I must admit, I really wasn't looking forward to spending my Saturday learning how to memorize Scripture, but it turned out to be the beginning of a great journey for me and helped me not only memorize Bible verses, but also facts and information throughout my college years. I remember during sorority pledging we were required to memorize our pledge book and all the information about each of the hundred or so sorority members, including their hometowns, their majors, and even the names of their boyfriends. This would probably be considered hazing now, but back then, it was just normal practice. My pledge sisters were slightly jealous because I was able to memorize it all quickly and easily. I did it using the method I learned at the Scripture memory conference with my dad.

Basically, the key tool was to use crazy, funny pictures to represent words. Our minds tend to remember pictures better than they remember words, so if you can turn a verse into a picture, it helps to seal it in your memory. Let me show you what I mean. Let's learn Hebrews 10:24 together. Whenever you start to learn a verse, I encourage you to write it down either in a notebook or on an index card. Say the verse aloud and think about what it is saying. Here's the verse:

> Let us consider how we may spur one another on toward
> love and good deeds.

Now we are going to draw silly pictures to help us remember the words. You may enjoy this method of memorizing or you may not. Stick with me and try it just for this verse and see if it works for you. Trust me, you don't need to be a great artist to draw these pictures—simple little drawings work just fine. Okay, so are you ready? First, for the words "let us," draw a head of lettuce. Yes, that's right—a head of lettuce like you would use to make a salad. Remember, I said these pictures need to be crazy, because we are more likely to remember odd pictures than normal ones. Now draw a stick figure of a person with a striped prison suit on. Draw a jug of cider in his hand. You just drew a con (convicted criminal) with cider, which stands for *consider*. For the word *how* I would put a large question mark with an H on the top. See—now you have the first part of the verse in picture form: "Let us consider how..."

For the word *we*, I always draw a little playground slide because I think of kids saying "wheeeee" as they go down it. You may have another way you want to picture *we,* but that's the symbol I consistently use. Next is the word *may,* and I always draw a maypole. Over the years I've gotten to know my little signals very well, and I'm sure you will get to know yours too. I drew a maypole at the end of the slide. The next word in our verse is *spur,* so I drew cowboy spurs. It helps to connect the spurs to the maypole. Now remember these are really simple little drawings—nothing elaborate. I sketch just enough to help me begin to picture the silly drawings in my mind.

For *one another,* I drew a large number one and then another smaller one beside it. For the word *on* you can either draw an off/on switch or put an arrow pointing on and toward the rest of the verse. I used a heart to represent *love* and a helping hand to demonstrate *good deeds.* Here's how my crazy picture looked:

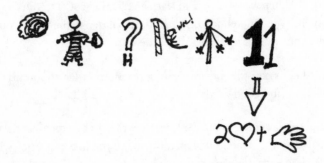

To help you remember the reference, you can draw pictures for that as well. You could think of a picture that you will use for each book of the Bible. For instance, for "Hebrews" you could draw a stick figure of a man brewing coffee (he brews). You can also think of a picture for each number (like a surfboard for the number ten, a Noah's ark for a two, and a golf club for a four). I find it helpful to write the number down and also look the verse up in my Bible so I see its placement in the chapter. (When I memorize a whole chapter, I typically don't memorize the individual verse numbers.)

Okay, so let's see if the drawings helped you. Take a look at your drawing one more time and say the verse aloud. Now look away and picture your drawing in your mind and say the verse again. How did you do? I like to use a notebook or index cards to write out the verse and draw the picture. Index cards work well because you can carry them with you throughout your day and refresh your memory. You may want to post them throughout your house. Now if you don't exactly like the picture-drawing method, that's okay—there are plenty of other ideas I want to share with you.

Reviewing and Accountability

Repetition, repetition, repetition! Reviewing the verse the next day is another important key to sealing it into your brain. Typically when I am learning a new verse, I will memorize it one day, and then the next morning I will try to say it, and usually I will have completely forgotten it! Do not be discouraged if this happens to you. And it most likely will—that's why reviewing it the next day is essential. I have found that instead of getting frustrated with myself, if I will simply review the verse again the very next day, then I've got it. The tough part is to remain consistent in reviewing. Consistency can be hard for all of us; I know—I'm the Queen of Inconsistency.

It all comes down to forming habits that become second nature to you, like brushing your teeth or turning on the coffee machine in the morning. Every morning I have a certain routine, and you probably do too. One part of that routine is while I'm sipping on that first cup of coffee in the morning, I write down several of the things I'm thankful for from the past day. Since I have my notebook open, I review my memory verse from the day before and then write down my new verse along with the cute/crazy pictures. It's a good idea to review the verse again right before you go to sleep at night.

Once I have learned a new passage of Scripture, I continue to review it daily for two or three weeks. This helps me seal the passage into my long-term memory. Once I really know a passage and can say it without hesitation, then I put it in a notebook to review it once a week (instead of daily). I encourage you to have a regular way to review the old passages you have already memorized, so you don't forget them. I keep a three-ring binder with tabbed sections for each day of the week. I review several passages in Psalms on Mondays, 1 John on Tuesdays, Colossians on Wednesdays,

Philippians on Thursdays, and several chapters in Romans on Fridays. I have a copy of each passage I have memorized in the notebook under daily sections, so that if I've forgotten a few words I can refresh my memory.

I also find it helpful to review the passages by saying them audibly. Perhaps while you are driving to work, or right after the kids have gone to school, or while you are doing laundry or working out will be the best time. For me, the best time is while I'm exercising in the morning. My brain is always more alert when I am working out, and I have found that the rhythm helps me think more clearly. What about you? When is a good time for you to work on a new verse and review old ones? Write your plan in the lines below:

I plan to work on new memory verses (when?):

_____

I plan to review my past memory work (when?):

_____

How do you stay motivated? This is where accountability is key. Remember when I told you about the family friend who challenged me? I want you to know that without the challenge of this friend, I would have wandered away, given up, or lost interest. But because I knew we would have to meet and recite in front of our spouses over dinner, I was motivated. When you have someone who is going to ask you if you have been keeping up with your memory work or ask to hear it, then it helps you stay a little more consistent than if you are trying to do it on your own. Stop and think of one person who may be interested in being your accountability partner. It helps if it is someone who is interested in memorizing Scripture too—then you can say your passages to each other. Have you thought of someone? Write their name below:

My accountability partner could be:

_____

Now don't be afraid to ask her. Honestly, this may be your first and most important step toward starting a personal memorization program. If you will make the effort to ask someone to meet with you and actually set a date on the calendar for your first meeting, you have made a huge step to getting the job done. So right now, put down this book and contact the person whose name you wrote on the line above. Set a time to meet several weeks from now to go over your first passage. It doesn't matter if it is one verse, a few verses, or an entire chapter. Take the first step by setting up a time to recite it. Write the time and date for your first accountability meeting here:

We will meet on _____ (day)

at _____ (time).

More Secrets to Memorizing Scripture

Learning the order of the books of the Bible was always a little difficult for me as a kid. I really wanted to know them so I wouldn't look like an idiot trying to fumble around in my Bible while everyone else had their finger on the passage at Sunday school. The trick that helped me the most was learning short songs that contained all the books of the Bible in order. Singing them helped me learn them quickly, and I still sing those songs in my head when I'm trying to find a book like Zephaniah or Haggai. There are several music CDs for kids that are specifically created to help them hide God's Word in their hearts. Music helps us memorize items because it incorporates rhythm and sound. I'm impressed with how many moms I know who tell me they learned Scripture as they listened to the music CDs with their kids in the car. One group that creates music for the express purpose of hiding God's Word in your heart is a group called Seeds. Go to www.seedsfamilyworship.com to order their CDs.

The more you can incorporate all of your senses, the easier it is to memorize. When you say the words aloud, you are not only speaking them, you also hear them. When you write the verse out and draw funny pictures you are using visual stimulation. Additionally, sometimes I will make up hand motions to go along with a verse, incorporating a little kinesthetic learning. If you like sentence structure and patterns, another memorization tool you can use is breaking the verse into phrases as well as connecting words that start with the same letter or have the same word repeated throughout the verse. For instance, Romans 8:5 reads,

> Those who live according to the flesh have their minds set on what the flesh desires; but those who live in accordance with the Spirit have their minds set on what the Spirit desires.

Notice the repeated words and phrases. It helps me to rewrite the verse in a structured way, emphasizing the repeated phrases and words by circling or boxing them in like this:

> *Those who* <u>*live*</u> *according to the* <u>*flesh*</u>
> **have their** <u>**minds**</u> **set on what** *the* <u>*flesh*</u> *desires;*
> *but*
> *those who* <u>*live*</u> *in accordance with the* <u>*Spirit*</u>
> **have their** <u>**minds**</u> **set on what** *the* <u>*Spirit*</u> *desires.*

I have one friend who memorized several chapters of Scripture by writing out a verse every day until she learned it. Boy, did she have a lot of spiral notebooks! I think she cleaned out the school-supply section at Walmart. She had notebooks full of Scripture she had written again and again, and this method worked great for her in retaining the Scripture in her memory. If possible, try to work the Scripture into your conversation with someone during the day. This keeps you thinking about the verse and looking for ways to apply it to your daily life.

My friend Caroline Boykin wrote a great book called *The Well-Versed Family*, in which she offers inspiration and helpful tips in memorizing Scripture. I love her practical, doable ideas for both families and individuals. Some of her tips include posting sticky notes on the bathroom mirrors with one word on each note, then slowly taking away the notes one word at time. You can also do this with a whiteboard (writing the verse out and erasing different words until the verse is learned). Caroline also recommends a Rolodex file of memory verses so you can flip to a new verse or passage each day for review, and even doing a video recording of your family reciting verses, which gives your family a fun way to review. She has many creative tips, so I encourage you to go to her website at www.wellversedliving.com.

What to Memorize

When I was a kid, my parents loved to take us to Barnhill's Restaurant in Akron, Ohio. It was our favorite place because the entrance of the store was filled with barrels and bins of every kind of candy you can imagine. After dinner, our parents would give us a certain amount of money to spend on candy, and we had a blast figuring how we wanted to spend our money. It was overwhelming! How do you choose when there are so many options? Well, that's the way you may feel about choosing what verses and passages you want to memorize. There's so many good, rich passages that it's almost impossible to know where to start.

I'll tell you a few of my favorites, but more important, I encourage you to begin keeping your own list of passages as you read God's Word. I have chosen seven passages I say aloud every single morning. You will see that I use different translations for different passages. Generally I like to memorize in the New International Version, but sometimes I will memorize in the New Living Translation or the English Standard Version. My daily passages are as follows:

> *Psalm 37:23-24* (NLT)
> The Lord directs the steps of the godly.
> > He delights in every detail of their lives.
> Though they stumble, they will never fall,
> > for the Lord holds them by the hand.

> *Psalm 62:5-8*
> Let all that I am wait quietly before God,
> > for my hope is in him.
> He alone is my rock and my salvation,
> > my fortress where I will not be shaken.
> My victory and honor come from God alone.
> > He is my refuge, a rock where no enemy can reach me.
> O my people, trust in him at all times.
> > Pour out your heart to him,
> > for God is our refuge.

John 15:5
"I am the vine; you are the branches. If you remain in me and I in you, you will bear much fruit; apart from me you can do nothing."

Ephesians 3:16-21
I pray that out of his glorious riches he may strengthen you with power through his Spirit in your inner being, so that Christ may dwell in your hearts through faith. And I pray that you, being rooted and established in love, may have power, together with all the Lord's holy people, to grasp how wide and long and high and deep is the love of Christ, and to know this love that surpasses knowledge—that you may be filled to the measure of all the fullness of God.

Now to him who is able to do immeasurably more than all we ask or imagine, according to his power that is at work within us, to him be glory in the church and in Christ Jesus throughout all generations, for ever and ever! Amen.

Psalm 23 (NLT)
The LORD is my shepherd;
    I have all that I need.
He lets me rest in green meadows;
    he leads me beside peaceful streams.
    He renews my strength.
He guides me along right paths,
    bringing honor to his name.
Even when I walk
    through the darkest valley,
I will not be afraid,
    for you are close beside me.
Your rod and your staff
    protect and comfort me.
You prepare a feast for me
    in the presence of my enemies.

You honor me by anointing my head with oil.
My cup overflows with blessings.
Surely your goodness and unfailing love will pursue me
all the days of my life,
and I will live in the house of the LORD
forever.

Hebrews 10:23-25
Let us hold unswervingly to the hope we profess, for he who promised is faithful. And let us consider how we may spur one another on toward love and good deeds, not giving up meeting together, as some are in the habit of doing, but encouraging one another—and all the more as you see the Day approaching.

2 Peter 1:3-4 (NLT)
By his divine power, God has given us everything we need for living a godly life. We have received all of this by coming to know him, the one who called us to himself by means of his marvelous glory and excellence. And because of his glory and excellence, he has given us great and precious promises. These are the promises that enable you to share his divine nature and escape the world's corruption caused by human desires.

You may want to look at section E in the back of this book, entitled "Where to Go in the Bible for Strength and Comfort," and choose additional verses to memorize. One of the greatest blessings of Scripture memory for me actually occurs in the middle of the night. I'm sure you know the feeling when you wake up and can't seem to get back to sleep. That's when all the cares and worries of your life start creeping in and overtaking your mind if you let them. Thankfully, when you have memorized Scripture you can get rid of the worries by quoting God's Word while you are lying there in bed. I fall back to sleep with a peace that passes all understanding. Isaiah 26:3 reminds us that God will keep in perfect peace those whose minds are stayed on Him.

Another great advantage to memorizing Scripture is that it helps us stand firm against temptation. Pastor and author Chuck Swindoll says, "While there is no quick and easy cure-all, I do believe that one particular discipline (more than any other) will break the world's attempts to mold our minds: Memorizing Scripture."[3] May we be diligent to fill our minds and hearts with God's truth. Start with a verse. Then, why not move on to memorize a chapter? And then go ahead, memorize the entire book! Believe it is possible. Ask for God's direction and help, and let Him lead you to the method that works best for you. He is our Helper and Guide.

Digging Deeper

Choose one passage to memorize, and write it out in your journal. Let your accountability partner know about it and get started. You can do it!

DISCUSS

1. What are some of the benefits of memorizing Scripture?

2. What are some of the specific reasons you struggle with Scripture memory?

3. What are ways you can overcome each of these struggles?

HELPFUL RESOURCES

Helpful online resources and phone apps for Bible memory:

- www.memlok.com
- http://learnscripture.net
- www.memverse.com
- http://scripturetyper.com
- www.mobilizefaith.com

Woman of the Word

Jennifer grew up in the church, but it wasn't until she faced personal tragedy and loss that the Word became real to her. Here she shares her story.

The steps along the journey to becoming a woman of the Word are divinely orchestrated for each person. My journey began when I was eight years old attending a small rural church in western Kentucky. I grew up in a Christian home attending church and going to youth group every week; in Sunday school I was taught the gospel, in youth group we were challenged with Bible drills, and our pastor always encouraged Scripture memorization. Although my church involvement was active, my growth in God's Word was not. Little did I know that a foundation of biblical principles was being laid that one day would prove to be invaluable.

Knowing God's Word intimately became my utmost desire during a time in my life where I desperately needed courage, strength, and understanding. In the summer of 1993, two and half months from my wedding day, tragedy jolted me out of my biblical slumber. The corporate airplane my fiancé was piloting crashed, killing all on board as well as my hopes and dreams.

During the sleepless and tearful nights following the accident, God so graciously comforted me with His Scripture. Words penned by man but breathed by God gave me courage and strength to navigate each day. I found hope in the New Testament where John records the words spoken by Jesus: "You will grieve, but your grief will turn to joy…and no one will take away your joy" (John 16:20,22). I found courage by reading about the Israelites' journey to the Promised Land and God's assurance to Joshua that He would never leave him nor forsake him (Joshua 1:4). I found comfort from the words written by the Old

Testament prophet Jeremiah: "Because of the LORD's great love we are not consumed, for his compassions never fail. They are new every morning, great is your faithfulness" (Lamentations 3:22-23).

Yes, great is His faithfulness; God faithfully and mercifully guided me back to His Word and the biblical foundation of my childhood. You see, as I spent more time in the presence of God reading His Word, He soothed my hurting heart as only He could with compassion, grace, and love. With healing came a new excitement to meet Him within the pages of His Holy Word. I will never understand the "why" of such tragedies. That knowledge is for God alone, but I do know that understanding His grace only comes from spending time with Him.

Twenty years have passed since that dreadful day in June, and I have taken a lot of steps along the journey, yet the promise remains true: "We know that in all things God works for the good of those who love him, who have been called according to his purpose" (Romans 8:28). I'm grateful for a God who lovingly allowed blessings to follow tragedy by mending my broken heart and by generously giving me a new hope and future, and most importantly giving me an unquenchable desire to read His Holy Word. We never know where our journey will take us, but with Him as our guide the destination is sure to be heavenly!

Part Two

Loving the Bible

～

I delight in your decrees;
I will not neglect your word.

PSALMS 119:16

How precious is the Book divine,
By inspiration given!
Bright as a lamp its doctrines shine,
To guide our souls to heaven.

JOHN FAWCETT

From Genesis to Revelation, the Bible magnificently portrays God's unfailing love for His people. I marvel at the beauty of His plan and design as I see His Word paint a masterpiece of redemption and grace on every page. My deepest desire is for you to experience His great love for you in a very real way.

Each chapter in this part invites you to make a heart connection with God as you observe the depiction of His love in living and vibrant color—from the big picture of the Bible to God's "favorite color" to His covenant of love. You will see that His Spirit is a gift of love to all believers in Christ, and you will also spend time considering seven of the most loving words ever uttered.

The more I read the Bible, the more I realize I am just beginning to understand God's amazing attributes and His grace and mercy toward us. His love and affection draw us to Him. My heart hungers to know more about Him and understand His love as it is revealed in the Scriptures. I hope these chapters will stir that hunger in your heart as well, creating an indescribable and unquenchable delight in and longing for His Word.

6

The Big Picture

In the past God spoke to our ancestors
through the prophets at many times
and in various ways, but in these last days
he has spoken to us by his Son, whom he appointed
heir of all things, and through whom also he made the universe.

HEBREWS 1:1-2

The Word is like a glorious choir,
And loud its anthems ring;
Though many parts and tongues unite,
It is one song they sing.

EDWIN HODDER

Are you familiar with Vincent van Gogh's painting *Starry Night*? I recently had the opportunity to see it at the Museum of Modern Art (MOMA) in New York City and was struck by its quiet simplicity and dramatic color. I stood and stared at it for a while, thinking about the artist's difficult life and trying to understand what he was attempting to portray in this masterpiece. Later I read up on Van Gogh and found out that at an early age he was deeply religious and spent his younger years reaching out to the impoverished with the message of the gospel. As he grew as an artist, he experienced rejection from the art community and was often characterized by his critics as sloppy, crude, and childish.

Most of us remember his ear-cutting incident, which occurred after a fight with his artist friend Paul Gauguin. I must admit I've always thought of Van Gogh as "that crazy artist." Yet as I read about his life, I saw a different side. It was while he was in the mental hospital that he painted *Starry Night*, possibly portraying his feelings of isolation and pain. The prominent features in this painting are the moon, 11 stars, a large dark cypress tree on the left, and a church as the centerpiece. Both the church and the tree point up toward heaven. Many art scholars believe there is a deeper religious meaning within the painting. The 11 stars can be linked with the story of Joseph, one of the 12 sons of Jacob in the Old Testament.

Joseph was also an outcast who experienced imprisonment and rejection. He had a dream in which 11 stars bowed down to his 1 star. The stars in Joseph's dream represented his accusing brothers, while the stars in Van Gogh's painting most likely represented those critics who preferred the "beautiful and realistic" art of his day. Like Joseph in the Bible, Van Gogh was both a dreamer and an outcast. The interesting thing is that the painting is almost prophetic, because just as God turned the tables and allowed Joseph to rise above his circumstances to become second in command in Egypt, so Van Gogh gained worldwide fame (although posthumously) as a gifted and renowned artist. Isn't it amazing to discover the hidden treasures within a painting if you really take the time to see them?

Most artwork invites us to ponder its deeper meaning, but we rarely take the time to stop and observe it. In order to really see the intent of the artist we have to step back and take an intentional look at the work as a whole, to get a feel for the big picture. What is the artist trying to say? What textures and strokes is he using to portray a message or a concept? How does he use light and color? What is he revealing about himself?

In a similar way, as we take time to observe the magnificent masterpiece of the Bible, we learn what the Great Artist reveals about Himself. We can discover the different aspects of His nature and understand His love for us. His colorful and divine work is vibrant with personal stories, eternal wisdom, and grace-filled redemption, all painted on the canvas of His unfailing love. We learn about His nature as we observe His hand at work from the creation to the promise of the Messiah. Most important, we see the portrait of His Son hidden within every brushstroke of this divinely inspired book.

God has revealed Himself to us through the powerful masterpiece of His Word. And just as we may stand and stare at a painting in a museum, studying every aspect of it—as I did with the *Starry Night*—so we must look intently into His perfect book. Let's step back and take the opportunity to observe the divine Artist's handiwork as a whole, looking at the big picture and considering the flow of His message.

The masterpiece of the Bible is composed of 66 books, all fitting perfectly together with miraculous precision. There is no other book like it in all the world of literature. Over 40 writers, each moved by the Holy Spirit. Think about it—66 books, written by 40 different authors over a period of 1500 years, in three different languages, on three different continents! Further, all the books have a common theme of God's universal love for all humanity and a common message that He has provided salvation to His people through His Son, Jesus. That couldn't just happen. We couldn't even try to make that happen. It was orchestrated and designed by God through His Spirit so that the entire picture of the Bible points to Christ. The apostle Peter confirmed the divine inspiration of the Scriptures by painting a starry night picture himself when he wrote:

> We also have the prophetic message as something completely reliable, and you will do well to pay attention to it, as to a light shining in a dark place, until the day dawns and the morning star rises in your hearts. Above all, you must understand that no prophecy of Scripture came about by the prophet's own interpretation of things. For prophecy never had its origin in the human will, but prophets, though human, spoke from God as they were carried along by the Holy Spirit (2 Peter 1:19-21).

In each book of the Bible, God unfolds the plan of redemption and progressively paints a clearer image of Christ as we move from the Old Testament to the New. Two kingdoms are portrayed throughout Scripture: the kingdom of light and the kingdom of darkness. How wonderful to know that as believers in Christ, He has rescued us from the kingdom of darkness and brought us into the kingdom of light (Colossians 1:12-13). The contrast between darkness and light is evident throughout the masterpiece of God's Word from beginning to end.

The Old Testament reveals God's attributes and helps us understand His unfailing love for His people. The Great Artist has always had a plan for His people, and He paints a beautiful picture of redemption in the Old Testament giving us impressions and glimpses of the coming Messiah. There are 39 books in the Old Testament, written in a span of approximately 1000 years. Don't let the word *Old* fool you. It's tempting to see the word *Old* and think outdated or something you can't relate to. That's the amazing thing about the Bible. Every time I read it, I learn fresh truths that apply to my life today. More importantly, I learn about the timeless and unchanging attributes of Almighty God.

The Old Testament can be divided into five sections as follows:

- *The Pentateuch* (Hebrew *Torah*): Genesis, Exodus, Leviticus, Numbers, Deuteronomy (*Pentateuch* means five scrolls)
- *Historical Books*: Joshua, Judges, Ruth, 1 and 2 Samuel, 1 and 2 Kings, 1 and 2 Chronicles, Ezra, Nehemiah, Esther
- *Poetic Books*: Job, Psalms, Proverbs, Ecclesiastes, Song of Songs
- *Major Prophets*: Isaiah, Jeremiah, Lamentations, Ezekiel, Daniel
- *Minor Prophets*: Hosea, Joel, Amos, Obadiah, Jonah, Micah, Nahum, Habakkuk, Zephaniah, Haggai, Zechariah, Malachi

When I think of the glorious way the Old Testament flows together, it reminds me of a beautiful impressionist painting, providing impressions of the coming Messiah. Each story and each message from creation to the Minor Prophets fit together, revealing a bigger picture of God's plan. Every story points to the one big story. The illustration God is giving us on every page is the fact that He is the One who provides redemption. We are powerless to save ourselves, but He is mighty to save His people.

After the last Old Testament prophet, Malachi, penned his message, the Holy Spirit was silent for over 400 years, until the time of Christ. The impressions were undeniable, yet the mystery of Christ was not yet revealed. The New Testament brings God's redemptive plan into clear focus through the reality of Jesus Christ.

A Perfect Portrait

A seemingly insignificant encounter with a reprint of Rembrandt's painting *The Return of the Prodigal* set in motion a spiritual adventure for author Henri Nouwen. After observing the picture, Nouwen recounted,

> Rembrandt's embrace remained imprinted on my soul far more profoundly than any temporary expression of

emotional support. It had brought me into touch with something within me that lies far beyond the ups and downs of a busy life, something that represents the ongoing yearning of the human spirit, the yearning for a final return, an unambiguous sense of safety, a lasting home.[1]

Wow, when's the last time a picture moved you to that extent?

Years later Nouwen had the opportunity to visit the Hermitage Museum in St. Petersburg, Russia, to see the original painting. Amid the tourists coming and going, he sat himself down in a red velvet chair in front of the painting and stayed there for hours, staring at the details while pondering Christ's parable (not too different than my staring at *Starry Night* at the MOMA). Nouwen studied the picture from every angle, considering the humility of the prodigal, the love of the father, and the resentment of the other son. The realism and emotion of each character in the painting drew him to consider every aspect of the parable and how it related to his own life.

In his book *The Return of the Prodigal Son,* Nouwen explores the challenge to love as the father and to receive love as the son. He wrote,

> I am the prodigal son every time I search for unconditional love where it cannot be found. Why do I keep ignoring the place of true love and persist in looking for it elsewhere? Why do I keep leaving home where I am called a child of God, the Beloved of my Father?[2]

Rembrandt's depiction of the parable was expressed with such clarity that the reality had a profound effect on Nouwen's life. Similarly, as we gaze into the New Testament, we discover Christ with such clarity that the reality of who He is can't help but have a life-changing impact on our lives.

Let's take a moment (like Nouwen) to step back and take a look at the portrait of Christ found in New Testament. The masterpiece of the New Testament is composed of 27 books and is usually separated into the following five divisions:

- *The Gospels*: Matthew, Mark, Luke, and John
- *The spreading of the gospel/history*: Acts

- *Paul's epistles*: Romans, 1 and 2 Corinthians, Galatians, Ephesians, Philippians, Colossians, 1 and 2 Thessalonians, 1 and 2 Timothy, Titus, and Philemon
- *General epistles*: Hebrews, James, 1 and 2 Peter, 1, 2 and 3 John, Jude
- *Apocalyptic literature/prophecy*: Revelation

God used the writers of the New Testament to paint the picture of Christ with intense realism. Hebrews expresses this mystery made clear:

> In the past God spoke to our ancestors through the prophets at many times and in various ways, but in these last days he has spoken to us by his Son, whom he appointed heir of all things, and through whom also he made the universe. The Son is the radiance of God's glory and the exact representation of his being, sustaining all things by his powerful word (Hebrews 1:1-3).

The Gospels paint the picture of Christ from four different perspectives, bringing God's mysterious plan of redemption into full and vibrant clarity. Jesus Christ is the fulfillment of all that was mysteriously portrayed in the Old Testament. This was God's plan from the beginning of time. Paul wrote to the Ephesians, "He chose us in him before the creation of the world to be holy and blameless in his sight." He went on to write,

> God has now revealed to us his mysterious plan regarding Christ, a plan to fulfill his own good pleasure. And this is the plan: At the right time he will bring everything together under the authority of Christ—everything in heaven and on earth. Furthermore, because we are united with Christ, we have received an inheritance from God, for he chose us in advance, and he makes everything work out according to his plan (Ephesians 1:9-11 NLT).

Just as a great and skillful artist plans out his painting or sculpture in order to create a masterpiece, so God, the Great Artist, created a beautiful plan of redemption for His people. Again in Ephesians we read,

You were dead in your transgressions and sins, in which you used to live when you followed the ways of this world and of the ruler of the kingdom of the air, the spirit who is now at work in those who are disobedient. All of us also lived among them at one time, gratifying the cravings of our flesh and following its desires and thoughts. Like the rest, we were by nature deserving of wrath. But because of his great love for us, God, who is rich in mercy, made us alive with Christ even when we were dead in transgressions—it is by grace you have been saved. And God raised us up with Christ and seated us with him in the heavenly realms in Christ Jesus, in order that in the coming ages he might show the incomparable riches of his grace, expressed in his kindness to us in Christ Jesus. For it is by grace you have been saved, through faith—and this is not from yourselves, it is the gift of God—not by works, so that no one can boast. For we are God's handiwork, created in Christ Jesus to do good works, which God prepared in advance for us to do (Ephesians 2:1-10).

Like the prodigal son, we have all sinned and gone our own way, yet God opened His arms of love toward us. We are saved by His grace through faith in Christ. It is not by our works, but by His work on the cross! My friend, have you placed your faith in God's plan, His Son, Jesus Christ? The purpose of the Bible is to point to Him. Paul wrote, "There is one God and one mediator between God and mankind, the man Christ Jesus" (1 Timothy 2:5). Because God loves us, He provided a way to redeem us to Himself. This is why Jesus came. This is why He died on the cross. In the next chapter we will be talking about the most beautiful color in the Bible, the crimson color of His blood shed for us. (If you would like to talk to someone about placing your faith in Christ, I encourage you to call 1-888-Need-Him or go to www.ChatAboutJesus.com.)

Finally, I want to point out how wonderful it is to know we are His precious handiwork, as Paul wrote in the Ephesians passage we just read. The word Paul used for *handiwork* (Greek *poiema*) means "workmanship" or "masterpiece." Yes, God has had a redemptive plan throughout the ages, and God has a specific plan for your life as well. He has created us for a purpose here in this world, and He planned it long ago. We are His masterpiece! What an amazing truth. Reflect on it and thank the Lord for the mighty work He is continuing to do in your life. Remember, "He who began a good work in you will carry it on to completion until the day of Christ Jesus" (Philippians 1:6). Your life is an unfinished masterpiece, but take heart, for we know the Great Artist has a perfect plan!

Digging Deeper

Read Ephesians 1–2. Write down all God teaches you about His divine plan for both you personally and for His people.

DISCUSS

1. Why would you say the Bible could be defined as a masterpiece?

2. What are some ways you have seen the Divine Artist's hand at work in your life?

3. How does it comfort and strengthen you to know that you are God's handiwork (His masterpiece) and that He has a plan for your life?

HELPFUL RESOURCES

- *Dust to Glory: An Overview of the Bible* by R.C. Sproul
- *A Quick Overview of the Bible* by Douglas A. Jacoby
- *Understanding Scripture* by John Piper

Bible Fact

The whole English Bible, divided into chapters and verses, first appeared in 1560 in what is known as the "Geneva Bible." It was so called because it was prepared by the Reformers in Geneva.

7

God's Favorite Color

The law requires that nearly everything be cleansed with blood,
and without the shedding of blood there is no forgiveness.

HEBREWS 9:22

How wonderful it is to trace the scarlet thread of the blood of Christ
woven throughout the Bible!
How much more wonderful to experience
its redemption personally.

ADRIAN ROGERS

*I*t's not too difficult to figure out which color is my favorite. A quick look around my house and you will find pink notebooks, pink pens, pink writing pads, and even a pink computer cover. Don't even get me started on the pink clothes in my closet or the pink purses on my shelf. When you like a certain color, it tends to show.

Have you ever thought about what God's favorite color is? It's not too difficult to figure out, since He has sprinkled it throughout the pages of His Word. The color of crimson appears over and over again, from the Garden of Eden to the cross of Christ. It is the beautifully symbolic color of His unfailing and sacrificial love for us.

Dr. W.A. Criswell refers to this powerful color in his sermon "The Scarlet Thread Through the Bible." On the evening of December 31, 1961, Dr. Criswell preached a sermon with this title, starting at 7:30 p.m. and ending at midnight! Imagine that in today's give-it-to-me-quick culture! The address highlighted the references to the blood of Christ throughout the Old and New Testament. Criswell's passion for preaching and his love for Christ poured through this powerful message and into the hearts of the listeners. He related God's glorious and beautiful redemptive plan from creation to the cross to Christ's return. Years later, I had the privilege of hearing Dr. Criswell preach a series of sermons based on this one famous sermon. I was a young teen at the time, but I have never forgotten the power and love of the message.

One of the central stories in the sermon came from the book of Joshua and the life of Rahab, a prostitute. Joshua sent spies to view the land, specifically the great walled city of Jericho. The spies went directly to the house of Rahab, a prostitute. Now before you get any ideas of what these spies were up to, the narrative never mentions any sexual relationship between Rahab and the spies. Most likely, her home was a kind of inn or common meeting place (kind of like the saloons you see in old Western movies), which makes it a logical place for the spies to gather their intel. Someone informed the king of Jericho that the spies were in town, so the king sent a message to Rahab telling her to bring out the men who had come to her to spy out the land.

Rahab hid the men on her roof and lied about their whereabouts. Then she came to the men and made a plea for her life based on her knowledge of the God of Israel.

> I know that the LORD has given you this land and that a great fear of you has fallen on us, so that all who live in this country are melting in fear because of you. We have heard how the LORD dried up the water of the Red Sea for you when you came out of Egypt…When we heard of it, our hearts melted in fear and everyone's courage failed because of you, for the LORD your God is God in heaven above and on the earth below.

> Now then, please swear to me by the LORD that you will show kindness to my family, because I have shown kindness to you. Give me a sure sign that you will spare the lives of my father and mother, my brothers and sisters, and all who belong to them—and that you will save us from death (Joshua 2:9-13).

Do you sense her fear as well as her faith? She feared destruction by the God of all creation, but she also had faith that she could be spared. Now here's where the scarlet cord comes in! The spies promised that no harm would come to Rahab or her family as long as she displayed a scarlet cord outside her window. She and her family would be saved, but only as long as they stayed inside the house with the scarlet cord visible. The spies kept their promise, and when Israel captured the city, Rahab's family was spared. Without the scarlet cord, she would have been doomed, yet by God's grace she was saved.

Scarlet Is the Color of God's Grace

Rahab is a fascinating woman whose name is mentioned several times in the New Testament. To me, the coolest part of her story is that she was part of the lineage of Jesus. Yes, a prostitute! In Matthew 1:5 we see that she married Salmon, an Israelite, and became the mother of Boaz. Now perhaps you remember that name—Boaz is the man who married Ruth. He was her kinsman-redeemer. And as you may know, King David was Boaz and Ruth's great-grandson. Rahab is also mentioned in Hebrews 11 in what is known as the Hall of Faith. The writer of Hebrews wrote, "By faith the prostitute Rahab, because she welcomed the spies, was not killed with those who were disobedient."

Rahab's story gives us a picture of God's grace. She was saved from destruction, but it wasn't because she was a person of merit or character. She lived in a city that was doomed, and she had a profession that was far from pure and wholesome. We could point out further wrongdoing if we wanted to add the fact that she lied and hid spies from her own government. Yet, she had faith. She was protected from devastation because she had enough faith in God to hang a scarlet cord in her window. It was not her merit that saved her, it was His grace, and the symbol of her protection was a red rope. The scarlet cord serves as a reminder to us of His grace and salvation through faith and not by our own merit.

This scarlet color—blood-red—symbolizes God's grace toward believers throughout Scripture. It began in Genesis after the first sin. For the first time, death entered the world. Remember, Adam and Eve tried to cover their sin with fig leaves, but God gave them animal skins to cover their nakedness. Sadly, blood had to be shed for their sin. In Hebrews we are reminded without the shedding of blood there is no remission of sin. Why is blood so important? In Leviticus God answers that question: "The life of a creature is in the blood, and I have given it to you to make atonement for yourselves on the altar; it is the blood that makes atonement for one's life" (Leviticus 17:11).

We don't have to travel much further in Scripture to find the next example of the importance of a blood sacrifice. In Genesis 4, we read where Cain and Abel (the sons of Adam and Eve) offered their sacrifices to God. Abel brought an animal sacrifice, but Cain brought the fruit of the ground. God was pleased with Abel's sacrifice, but not with Cain's. Perhaps you are thinking how mean or horrible God is to require the blood of an animal, but we must recognize how serious our sin is in His eyes. He is holy and does not take sin lightly, and He doesn't want us taking our sin lightly either. Blood is a life-giving essence and it must be shed for the atonement of sins.

Following the Thread

As we see this scarlet thread woven throughout the history of God's people, we find Noah in Genesis 8 offering a blood sacrifice as soon as he landed on dry ground in the ark:

> The LORD smelled the pleasing aroma and said in his heart:
> "Never again will I curse the ground because of humans,
> even though every inclination of the human heart is evil
> from childhood. And never again will I destroy all living
> creatures, as I have done" (Genesis 8:20-21).

I want you to notice a phrase in this passage from Genesis: "Every inclination of the human heart is evil from childhood." This is the reason we need God's grace. We are hopeless, just as hopeless as Rahab. We would all be destined for destruction if it were not for His grace toward us. The scarlet thread leads us to Abraham through whom God chose to bless and form a nation, a people all His own. Abraham took his son Isaac to Mount Moriah—and perhaps you remember the story. Isaac asks his father, "The fire and wood are here, but where is the lamb for the burnt offering?" Even as a boy, Isaac knew they needed a blood offering. In a test of faith, God had told Abraham to offer his son on the altar, yet just as he raised his knife, God intervened through the voice of the angel of the Lord:

"Do not lay a hand on the boy," he said. "Do not do anything to him. Now I know that you fear God, because you have not withheld from me your son, your only son."

Abraham looked up and there in a thicket he saw a ram caught by its horns. He went over and took the ram and sacrificed it as a burnt offering instead of his son (Genesis 22:12-13).

God provided that offering! What a beautiful picture of Christ. I can't help but think of John the Baptist who declared about Jesus, "Behold the lamb of God who takes away the sin of the world."

As we continue to follow the scarlet thread through the Old Testament, we come to the story of Moses and the mighty deliverance of the Israelites from captivity in Egypt. God sent ten plagues on the Egyptian people to convince Pharaoh to let His people go. The final plague, the worst of all, was the death of the firstborn child throughout the land, carried out by the death angel. The Israelites' only protection was to put the blood of a lamb on the two side posts and the lintel of the door of the house. Only with this symbol of blood (in the form of a cross) would they be protected. Here again the scarlet thread leads us to the picture of Christ:

The blood will be a sign for you on the houses where you are, and when I see the blood, I will pass over you. No destructive plague will touch you when I strike Egypt (Exodus 12:13).

God's people fell under the protection of the scarlet symbol, the blood of the lamb, so that their firstborn children would not face death.

As the Israelites victoriously left Egypt, God led them through the wilderness toward the Promised Land. Along the way, they came to Mount Sinai, where Moses went up and received the Ten Commandments from God, written with "the finger of God" on two stone tablets (Exodus 31:18). After receiving laws and reading them to the people, the covenant of the Law was confirmed by a blood sacrifice. The Bible tells us that after Moses read the Law to the people, they responded by saying they would do everything the Lord had said. Then Moses took the blood, sprinkled it on the people, and confirmed the covenant.

Author and preacher Andrew Murray wrote,

> It is by the blood alone, that man can be brought into covenant fellowship [with God]. That which had been foreshadowed at the gate of Eden, on Mount Ararat [by Noah], on Moriah [by Abraham], and in Egypt, was now confirmed at the foot of Sinai in a most solemn manner. Without blood there could be no access by sinful man to a Holy God. There is, however, a marked difference…On Moriah the life was redeemed by the shedding of blood. In Egypt it was sprinkled on the door posts of the houses; but at Sinai, it was sprinkled on the persons themselves. The contact was closer, the application more powerful.[1]

Sprinkled with Scarlet

Are you one of those people who are uncomfortable at the sight of blood? Most of us tend to feel a little queasy. I have a hard time watching movies filled with violent bloody scenes. What is it about blood that gets our attention and turns our stomachs? Perhaps it is because we know that something living is terribly hurt and has suffered pain in order for blood to be spurting out of their vessels.

When my son-in-law was in medical school he told me that there were always a few students who would fall over, out cold, when they observed their first surgery. He also showed me the glasses he had to wear in surgery to ensure that spurting blood didn't spatter into his eyes. Now can you imagine what it must have been like for the Israelites there at the bottom of Mount Sinai, standing there and having the blood sprinkled on their faces? Why do you think God instructed Moses to sprinkle the blood on the people? The symbolism once again points to Christ. It's interesting to look at the times when the word *sprinkle* is used in the Bible. You could do a whole study on the word, but I'll point out just a few places where it is found. In Isaiah 52 we see it used in a prophecy about Jesus:

> See, my servant will act wisely;
> he will be raised and lifted up and highly exalted.

Just as there were many who were appalled at him—
> his appearance was so disfigured beyond that of any
> human being
> and his form marred beyond human likeness—
so he will *sprinkle* many nations,
> and kings will shut their mouths because of him.
For what they were not told, they will see,
> and what they have not heard, they will understand
(Isaiah 52:13-15).

Do you see the blessing of the sprinkle? "He will sprinkle many nations." The atoning blood sprinkled for the sins of the people would extend beyond just the Israelites. In the New Testament, Hebrews refers to sprinkling as well:

> The blood of goats and bulls and the ashes of a heifer sprinkled on those who are ceremonially unclean sanctify them so that they are outwardly clean. How much more, then, will the blood of Christ, who through the eternal Spirit offered himself unblemished to God, cleanse our consciences from acts that lead to death, so that we may serve the living God!
>
> For this reason Christ is the mediator of a new covenant, that those who are called may receive the promised eternal inheritance—now that he has died as a ransom to set them free from the sins committed under the first covenant (Hebrews 9:13-15).

The beautiful weaving of the scarlet thread through the Old Testament shows its full pattern in the New Testament in the person of Jesus Christ. Physically speaking, our blood is essential to our lives. When we eat, food is absorbed into our bloodstream and delivered to cells via our blood for growth and nourishment. When we breathe, oxygen is absorbed into the bloodstream and carried to cells. The blood is the delivery system to our entire bodies. If part of our body is deprived of blood, it will die. Blood also washes away the toxins in our bodies. The blood coursing through our veins brings nourishment, oxygen, and cleansing.

Just as blood brings both life and cleansing to our physical bodies, so Christ's blood brings life and cleansing to us spiritually. Many years before Christ, the prophet Isaiah wrote, "Come now, let us reason togther, says the Lord: though your sins are like scarlet, they shall be as white as snow; though they are red like crimson, they shall become like wool" (Isaiah 1:18 ESV). The Bible tells us that we were separated from God because of our sins. When Adam and Eve sinned in the garden, all creation fell. Our spirits were dead, but the good news is that our spirits have been made alive through Christ. For us as believers, His blood paid the penalty for our sins (1 John 2:1) and it continues to purify us (1 John 1:7). The life is in the blood! There is power in the blood! *Thank You, Jesus, for shedding Your blood so that we could be cleansed and purified from all unrighteousness. Thank You, Jesus, for Your life-giving blood shed on the cross for us.* Scarlet is truly a beautiful color, isn't it? It's the color of love.

Digging Deeper

Read Colossians 1 and record in your journal everything you learn about Christ and about His blood that was shed for you.

DISCUSS

1. In what ways is Rahab's story similar to every believer's story?

2. How do you see God's plan of redemption woven in the fabric of the Old Testament and fulfilled in Christ?

3. What significance does Christ's blood have to you?

HELPFUL RESOURCES

- *The Scarlet Thread Through the Bible* by W.A. Criswell (an audio recording of this sermon is available at www.wacriswell .org)

- *Power in the Blood of Christ* by Jennifer Kennedy Dean

- *The Power of the Blood of Christ,* by Andrew Murray

8

Covenant of Love

He remembers his covenant forever,
the promise he made, for a thousand generations.

Psalm 105:8

Engraved as in eternal brass,
The mighty promise shines;
Nor can the powers of darkness erase
Those everlasting lines.

Isaac Watts

When Curt and I were married more than 30 years ago, I remember thinking that I was the "luckiest girl in the world" to be marrying such a strong, godly, wise, and handsome man. I felt so honored that Curt wanted to marry *me*. Above all the other women in the world, he had chosen to enter into the covenant of marriage with *me*! Yet, as grateful as I am for my relationship with Curt, it's far more overwhelming to think that Almighty God desires to enter into a covenant relationship with us—His people!

A covenant is a relationship of devotion and loyalty. It is an agreement between two parties, and yet more personal than a formal contract. In a covenant relationship there is a deep sense of allegiance based on promises from both sides. Our God is a covenant-making God and the Bible itself is a covenant document. The Old Testament and New Testament actually represent Old and New Covenants—in fact, "testament" is the Latin word for "covenant." As we get to know the Bible, we see that covenants were the primary way in which the relationship between God and His people was established. It is important for us to examine the covenants God made with His people in order to have a better understanding of how God deals with us. While there are many horizontal covenants throughout the Bible between people and even nations, the covenant between God and His people is the central focus of the whole book.

Isn't that a magnificent thought? God's desire is to be in a covenant relationship with us! This divine relationship is based on unfailing love, a covenant of love between the Lord and His chosen people. As we learn about His covenants and promises, we can live with confidence knowing that God keeps His promises. John Calvin said, "Whatever God can do, he unquestionably will do, if he has promised it." If He said it, He will surely do it. We can depend on His words.

· In this chapter we will explore several of the significant covenants and promises made throughout Scripture. Most important, we will see that Jesus is the fulfiller and the fulfillment of all the promises and covenants of the Bible. May our love for Him grow deeper still as we learn about God's loving covenants with His people.

The Strength and Beauty of a Covenant

The first appearance of the word *covenant* in the Bible is found in Genesis 6:18. God said to Noah, "I will establish my covenant with you, and you will enter the ark—you and your sons and your wife and your sons' wives with you." Yet even before Noah, God had developed a covenant relationship with His people—Adam and Eve in the Garden of Eden. "The Lord God commanded the man, 'You are free to eat from any tree in the garden; but you must not eat from the tree of the knowledge of good and evil, for when you eat from it you will certainly die'" (Genesis 2:16-17). The promise within this covenant with Adam was life and the condition was perfect obedience. Often this is referred to as the *covenant of works*. The consequence of breaking it was death. Yet God also promised that one day the seed of the woman (Jesus) would crush the head of the enemy (Genesis 3:15), and some refer to this as the *covenant of grace*, which is the overriding theme of the entire Bible.

God in His mercy and love for us knew that mankind would always struggle with works and would always fall short, so He promised to make a new covenant. I can't express to you the joy and love I feel as I write this chapter. As we come to understand God's promises, we can't help but be overwhelmed by His great love toward us. Let's begin our understanding by learning a few more details about a blood covenant so we can get a picture of the depths of His love and commitment toward His people.

The Hebrew word for *covenant* is *berith,* which actually means "to cut" or "divide." This refers to the blood that had to be shed to bind the parties who were involved in the covenant. A blood covenant was not to be taken lightly—in fact in the ancient Hebrew culture (and in surrounding cultures), when two parties entered into a covenant, they engaged in a ceremony that typically involved a feast and several steps of ratification. Although it may seem foreign to us, in ancient times it was common among many of the cultures of the Middle East to ratify a covenant or an agreement in a very solemn and serious ceremony with some or all of the following steps:

1. *Exchange coats or robes.* Generally speaking, the outer coat represented the person himself. When a man offered his coat it was as if he was offering his very life.

2. *Remove belts.* The belt contained the weapons of warfare, so to take it off was symbolically showing that "your battles are my battles."

3. *Cut an animal in half.* This was known as "cutting the covenant." An animal was killed and cut down the middle and the two halves were placed opposite each other. Then each party would pass between the two halves. The implication was, "May God do so to me and more if I break this covenant."

4. *Raise the right arm and cut the palm of the hand, then clasp each other's hand to mingle the blood.* This is saying to the covenant partner, "We are becoming one with each other." Since the life is in the blood, to mingle blood means to intermingle the very life of both people.

5. *Exchange names.* Each person took part of the other person's name and incorporated it into their own to symbolize their newly established bond.

6. *Make a scar.* This would create an outward, permanent evidence of the covenant relationship. Often the covenant makers would rub the cut in their hand to make the scar, so that if someone wanted to fight one of the covenant partners, they would see that there was another they must fight as well.

7. *Identify assets.* They gave the terms of the covenant before a witness, listing all their assets and liabilities. They declared together, "From now on all that I own is yours." If something happened to one, the covenant partner would see that the wife and children were taken care of.

8. *Share a memorial meal.* They cooked the flesh of the sacrificed animal and ate it together.

9. *Plant a memorial tree.* They planted a tree as a symbol of their covenant and sprinkled the blood of the sacrificed animal on it.

Are you getting a picture of how serious a covenant was between two people or two groups? Today, we don't use the term *covenant* in our everyday lives and so we don't typically grasp the significance of this kind of bond. A covenant was filled with promises. Look over these nine steps again and think about how closely they relate to the marriage vows or the covenant of marriage. The exchange of names as well as the declaration "All that is mine is yours, and all that is yours is mine" reflect so beautifully the relationship between husband and wife. Oh, if only couples today recognized the importance of this covenant relationship! It is a bond that was not meant to be easily broken. And of course in the New Testament Paul relates the relationship of marriage to the relationship between Christ and His followers.

The Abrahamic Covenant

We find many of the above steps in the covenant God established with Abraham. In Genesis we read God's promise to Abram (his name would be changed to Abraham as a symbol of the covenant):

> The Lord had said to Abram, "Go from your country,
> your people and your father's household to the land I will
> show you.
> "I will make you into a great nation,
>   and I will bless you;
> I will make your name great,
>   and you will be a blessing.
> I will bless those who bless you,
>   and whoever curses you I will curse;

and all peoples on earth
      will be blessed through you" (Genesis 12:1-3).

Now this promise must have been shocking to Abram for a number of reasons, one of which was that his wife Sarai was barren (childless). Yet Abram obeyed God and stepped forward in faith. Notice the promise that "all peoples on earth will be blessed through you," once again pointing to Jesus. Later, in Genesis 15, we find God affirming His promises by reassuring Abram that his offspring would be as numerous as the stars in the sky. God confirmed the covenant by telling him to gather several animals and cut them in half. A deep sleep fell over Abram and a smoking firepot and flaming torch passed between the pieces, symbolizing the Lord's presence and demonstrating that all the obligations of the covenant would be ratified and fulfilled by God alone in the person of Jesus Christ. Interestingly, this was a one-sided covenant ceremony. Abram was asleep, again demonstrating that the full obligation of the covenant was God's.

In Genesis 17 we find another bloody covenant—circumcision. Why did God choose such a painful way for Abram to confirm the covenant? When you think about it, this is the most intimate and vulnerable part of a man. For a man to cut this part of his body gives the sense of complete dedication to God. Through this covenant of circumcision God announced that He was establishing an eternal covenant with Abram and his offspring. Abram would become the father of many nations, so God changed his name (remember step five) to *Abraham*.

The Mosaic Covenant

Another significant covenant in the Old Testament was the covenant God established with His people through Moses. In Exodus 34:28 we find the word *covenant* used when God gave the Ten Commandments to Moses on Mount Sinai: "He wrote on the tablets the words of the covenant—the Ten Commandments." The Israelites entered into a covenant with God, promising to observe and obey all the commandments. God's promise to them overflowed with loving-kindness:

If you obey me fully and keep my covenant, then out of
all nations you will be my treasured possession. Although
the whole earth is mine, you will be for me a kingdom of
priests and a holy nation (Exodus 19:5-6).

A treasured possession! Set apart as His special people! Oh, how blessed and rich they must have felt to have the God of all creation make such a pledge of love and loyalty to them! They responded by saying, "All that the LORD has spoken, we will do." They didn't propose the terms of the agreement; they simply responded to the covenant God made with them. Vern Poythress of Westminster Theological Seminary writes,

> When God makes a covenant with man, God is the sovereign, so he specifies the obligations on both sides. "I will be their God" is the fundamental obligation on God's side, while "they will be my people," is the fundamental obligation on the human side…The obligations on the human side of the covenants are also related to Christ. Christ is fully man as well as fully God. As a man, he stands with his people on the human side. He fulfilled the obligations of God's covenants through his perfect obedience.[1]

God knew we could never fulfill our obligation for the covenant, so He fulfilled it for us through the death and resurrection of Christ. The Old Testament covenants with human obligations all point to Christ's achievement on the cross. God ratified and fulfilled the covenant, just as it was portrayed with Abraham. Christ changed our situation from being alienated from God to being His beloved children, Christ's beloved bride. Paul wrote to the Colossians, "Once you were alienated from God and were enemies in your minds because of your evil behavior. But now he has reconciled you by Christ's physical body through death to present you holy in his sight, without blemish and free from accusation" (Colossians 1:21-22). As followers of Christ, we are His treasured possession and His beloved bride. Stop to think of the love He has for us. Take a moment to thank Him and praise Him for allowing us to be His treasured possession.

The New Covenant

When I go grocery shopping, it always baffles me when I see the old regular detergent that I've always used, but right next to it is the same product, only it is labeled "New and Improved." Who would want the old stuff if you can have the new and improved stuff? Doesn't everyone want "New and Improved"? Well, apparently not. I suppose there are those stick-in-the-muds who still want the same thing they have been buying for 20 years. God provided a new and improved covenant to His people, but sadly, many were so attached to the Old Covenant with its rules and regulations that they didn't see the blessing of His New Covenant.

God prepared them and told them a new covenant was coming. Throughout the Old Testament, God spoke through His prophets and continually pointed to the New and definitely Improved Covenant. It wasn't just improved; it was perfect! Can you imagine seeing that label on a laundry detergent: "New and *Perfect*"? I suppose a perfect laundry detergent would get every stain out, no matter what—grape juice, chocolate, red Kool-Aid. All gone! That's what Christ did for us. He removed the stain of our sin completely, no matter how ugly and awful it was. In the Old Covenant, the sacrifice only covered over the stain of sin, but under the New Covenant Jesus removed the stain of sin completely. Perfect!

The prophet Jeremiah spoke of this New Covenant hundreds of years before Jesus was born:

> "The days are coming," declares the LORD,
>   "when I will make a *new covenant*
> with the people of Israel
>   and with the people of Judah.
>
> It will not be like the covenant
>   I made with their ancestors
> when I took them by the hand
>   to lead them out of Egypt,
> because they broke my covenant,
>   though I was a husband to them,"
> declares the LORD.
>   "This is the covenant I will make with the people of
>   Israel after that time," declares the LORD.
> "I will put my law in their minds
>   and write it on their hearts.
> I will be their God,
>   and they will be my people.
> No longer will they teach their neighbor,
>   or say to one another, 'Know the LORD,'

because they will all know me,
from the least of them to the greatest,"
declares the LORD.
"For I will forgive their wickedness
and will remember their sins no more"
(Jeremiah 31:31-35).

Doesn't that just give you goose bumps? Or as one of my friends calls them, "God bumps." How beautiful to think that Jesus Christ is the fulfillment of the New Covenant. Jesus made it perfectly clear that He was the promised Messiah and the fulfillment of this New Covenant. Reflect with me on His words at the Last Supper, the Passover meal: "This cup is the new covenant in my blood, which is poured out for you" (Luke 22:20). The writer of Hebrews summed it up: "For this reason Christ is the mediator of a new covenant, that those who are called may receive the promised eternal inheritance—now that he has died as a ransom to set them free from the sins committed under the first covenant" (Hebrews 9:15).

Completed

Are you a jigsaw-puzzle person? I've done a few in my lifetime. There is no better feeling than putting that last piece into place and declaring the puzzle finished, done, complete!

When Jesus declared, "It is finished" on the cross, there was great significance to the statement. He had accomplished the requirements of the covenant. The puzzle, the dilemma of sin, was completed on the cross and the stamp of approval was His resurrection. Think back to the nine steps involved in ratifying a blood covenant. Consider how Jesus fulfilled each requirement on our behalf:

1. Exchange coats or robes. Isaiah prophesied,

I delight greatly in the LORD;
my soul rejoices in my God.
For he has clothed me with garments of salvation
and arrayed me in a robe of his righteousness,

> as a bridegroom adorns his head like a priest,
>> and as a bride adorns herself with her jewels
> (Isaiah 61:10-11).

Remember what happened as Jesus approached the cross? The soldiers placed a crown of thorns and a purple robe on Him to mock Him. How interesting to think that He wore the robe on our behalf in order to clothe us with a robe of righteousness.

2. Remove belts. Removing the belt is similar to the laying down of weapons. It reminds me of Philippians 2 where Paul reflects Christ laying down his life for us:

> In your relationships with one another, have the same
> mindset as Christ Jesus:
> Who, being in very nature God,
>> did not consider equality with God
>> something to be used to his own advantage;
> rather, he made himself nothing
>> by taking the very nature of a servant,
>> being made in human likeness.
> And being found in appearance as a man,
>> he humbled himself
>> by becoming obedient to death—
>> even death on a cross!
> (Philippians 2:5-8).

3. Cut an animal in half. This broken body reminds me again of the Last Supper, where Jesus "took bread, gave thanks and broke it, and gave it to them, saying, 'This is my body given for you; do this in remembrance of me'" (Luke 22:19). And in 1 Corinthians 5:7 we are reminded that "Christ, our Passover lamb, has been sacrificed."

4. Raise the right arm and cut the palm of the hand. The symbolism is powerful here as we picture Christ's hands being nailed to the cross. His hands were pierced on our behalf. I don't know about you, but when I read that the participants of a covenant had to cut their palms, I shuddered to think how painful that must have been and how serious they were about the agreement. But Jesus went beyond simply cutting His hands—His hands were pierced through. He was serious about this covenant. He chose to suffer the pain on our behalf because He loves us so deeply.

5. Exchange names. The exchanging of names was significant because it implied the exchange of character, reputation, and authority. I am reminded of 1 Corinthians 5:17: "If anyone is in Christ, the new creation has come: The old has gone, the new is here!" When we trust Christ, we not only gain the name Christian, but we are literally regenerated. We become a new person in Christ. We are a part of His family, and His Spirit dwells within us, continually conforming us to the image of Christ. I'm also reminded that in Revelation 2:17 we find that we will be given a new name one day, "Whoever has ears, let them hear what the Spirit says to the churches. To the one who is victorious, I will give some of the hidden manna. I will also give that person a white stone with a new name written on it, known only to the one who receives it."

6. Make a scar. To me, this is the most endearing truth about Jesus. He chose to keep His scars. He didn't need to. In His glorified body, He could have been made completely whole and healed in every area, but He chose to keep the scars in His hands. Remember when He showed them to doubting Thomas? Why would Jesus choose to keep His scars? Perhaps as a symbolic reminder that we are His. Just as in the ancient covenant ritual, a scar allowed the enemy to see that there was an alliance formed, so Christ's scars are also a reminder to our enemy that we belong to Christ. He fights for us. God said to His people through the prophet Isaiah, "See, I have engraved you on the palms of my hands" (Isaiah 49:16). Yes, this was His plan long ago. The New Covenant would be marked in Jesus' hand.

7. Identify assets. He has given us so many great and precious promises, it is impossible to declare them all. Certainly the gift of eternal life and the gift of being a part of His family. Forgiveness of sins and the presence of the Holy Spirit. He is our Father and we can come to Him for anything.

Oh, what blessed and privileged children we are! Peter wrote, "His divine power has given us everything we need for a godly life through our knowledge of him who called us by his own glory and goodness. Through these he has given us his very great and precious promises, so that through them you may participate in the divine nature, having escaped the corruption in the world caused by evil desires" (2 Peter 1:3-4).

8. Share a memorial meal. It's interesting to think that Jesus celebrated a special Passover meal with His disciples in the Upper Room. Here He washed their feet, broke bread, and established the Lord's Supper confirming the New Covenant (Luke 22:20). We still observe this meal in remembrance of Him. Certainly this is a wonderful memorial meal, but there is a better one coming. In Revelation 19 the Marriage Supper of the Lamb is described, where Christ will be joined with His bride, the church.

9. Plant a memorial tree and sprinkle the sacrificed animal's blood on it. What a perfect image of the cross, planted in the ground with the Lamb of God's blood sprinkled on it. When we wear a cross, we are wearing that memorial tree as a symbol of what He did for us. Now He is at the right hand of the Father and is interceding for us and nothing can separate us from His love (Romans 8:34-35).

When I consider how Christ fulfilled the blood covenant, I stand in awe of our Holy and Perfect God. He knew exactly what He was doing from the very beginning of time, and He so beautifully pointed to His Son, Jesus Christ, throughout history. The Bible is overflowing with God's promises, but one common theme seems to flow throughout His Word: "I will be their God and they shall be my people." How wonderful to know that God keeps His promises. As believers in Christ, we have the assurance that we are His people, and that He is our Father. It is impossible to examine all of His promises in one chapter, but one thing is for certain: "All of God's promises have been fulfilled in Christ with a resounding 'Yes!'" as Paul wrote. He adds, "And through Christ, our 'Amen' [which means 'Yes'] ascends to God for his glory" (2 Corinthians 1:20 NLT).

Digging Deeper

Read Hebrews 8 and 9 and record all that you learn about God's covenant through Christ.

DISCUSS

1. How does it increase your love for God to know that He has made a covenant with His people?

2. Knowing what you have learned in this chapter about covenants, how does it make you feel secure in your relationship with Christ?

3. In what ways can you use the truths from this chapter to help someone who is afraid that they could lose their salvation?

HELPFUL RESOURCES

- *Our Covenant God: Living in the Security of His Unfailing Love* by Kay Arthur
- *Covenant Marriage* by Gary Chapman
- *Covenants of Promise* by Thomas Edward McComiskey

9

You Are Never Alone

*I will ask the Father, and he will give you
another advocate to help you and be with you forever.*

JOHN 14:16

*Come, Holy Spirit, God and Lord!
Be all thy graces now out-poured
On the believer's mind and soul,
To strengthen, save, and make us whole.*

MARTIN LUTHER

As a mother, I've found it's best to learn some things after the fact. For instance, take the time my daughter Grace called me from college and informed me that she had gone skydiving. It's probably best that I didn't know that ahead of time. Since she was calling me from her apartment and not from the emergency room, I figured she had survived without incident. I was a bit relieved to find out that she hadn't jumped out of the plane by herself. A seasoned skydiver was harnessed to her, so she was accompanied by an expert for the entire jump. Good to know she wouldn't have died alone! From the moment she took her leap of faith and jumped out of the plane to the second she touched down on solid ground, she was never alone.

In a similar way, as we take that first step of faith and place our trust in Christ, we are never alone. God has given us a wonderful helper, a comforter and teacher to guide us through this life until we safely land in our heavenly home. Just as the skydiver assured my daughter that he would help her and be with her the whole way, so the Lord has promised that we will never be alone, even in the darkest valleys. Paul wrote to believers in Christ, saying, "When you believed, you were marked in him with a seal, the promised Holy Spirit, who is a deposit guaranteeing our inheritance until the redemption of those who are God's possession—to the praise of his glory" (Ephesians 1:13-14).

Isn't it wonderful to know that God has given us His Spirit as a deposit, guaranteeing our inheritance? We are God's precious possession! His Spirit draws us to Him and gives us strength, wisdom, and power to live our daily lives. If God has given us such a wonderful helper, I want to know more about Him—don't you? Andrew Murray wrote, "For a healthy Christian life, it is indispensable that we should be fully conscious that we have received the Holy Spirit to dwell in us."[1] Just before Jesus went to the cross, He promised His disciples that they would not be left alone; rather, they would be given an advocate and helper:

> If you love me, keep my commands. And I will ask the Father, and he will give you another advocate to help you and be with you forever—the Spirit of truth. The world cannot accept him, because it neither sees him nor knows him. But you know him, for he lives with you and will be in you. I will not leave you as orphans; I will come to you. Before long, the world will not see me anymore, but you will see me. Because I live, you also will live. On that day you will realize that I am in my Father, and you are in me, and I am in you. Whoever has my commands and keeps them is the one who loves me. The one who loves me will be loved by my Father, and I too will love them and show myself to them (John 14:15-21).

Notice that this passage mentions each person in the Trinity—one God, yet three distinct persons. Most of us tend to reflect on God the Father with great reverence as we consider His holiness, His glory, and His love. We adore Jesus as our Savior and Lord, the Lamb of God who offered His life on our behalf. Oddly, though, when it comes to the Holy Spirit, many of us tend to want to keep at arm's length because we don't quite understand Him. Like a crazy family member that no one talks about, we tend to brush Him aside and refer to Him only on occasion.

But if we are to love and worship God with our whole heart, how can we leave out one-third of Him? Why would we want to brush aside part of the Godhead just because we are uncomfortable with Him or feel we don't understand Him? I want to know all of God, not just part of Him! Are you with me? Since God has given His Holy Spirit to each believer, then we need to get to know Him! So let's take a look at what the Bible tells us about the Holy Spirit.

The Spirit of God in the Old Testament

We find the first mention of the Holy Spirit in the second verse of the Bible, Genesis 1:2: "Now the earth was formless and empty, darkness was over the surface of the deep, and the Spirit of God was hovering over the waters." Isn't it amazing to think that the very same Spirit that hovered over the deep and brought order from chaos dwells within each believer in Christ? What a wonderful and comforting truth! In Job, the Holy Spirit is called the breath of the Almighty implying His life-giving power (Job 33:4). David wrote about the omnipresence of the Spirit of God in Psalm 139:7, saying, "Where can I go from your Spirit? Where can I flee from your presence?" The prophet Samuel said of God's Spirit that "the Glory of Israel does not lie or change his mind; for he is not a human being, that he should change his mind" (1 Samuel 15:29). Nehemiah referred to Him as God's "good Spirit," who will teach and lead us into all that is good.

In the Old Testament, God's Spirit came upon people and left them. The story I always think of is when Spirit of God rushed upon David as he was anointed as king (1 Samuel 16:13). But then in the very next verse we see that the Spirit departed from King Saul. To be clear, this has nothing to do with whether a person can lose their salvation, as it is not describing the role the Holy Spirit plays in the regeneration of a believer (which we find in the New Testament). It is rather about the empowering of the Holy Spirit in the lives of individuals in the Old Testament.

Isaiah spoke often of God's Spirit, calling Him the "Spirit of counsel" who gives us guidance, the "Spirit of might" who strengthens us, and the "Spirit of wisdom" who leads us into wisdom; He is the Spirit of knowledge who knows all things (Isaiah 11:2). Isaiah also calls Him the "Spirit of judgment," who discerns and divides good from evil (Isaiah 4:4; 28:6), and refers to Him as the "Spirit of the Sovereign Lord"—literally, "the Spirit of Yahweh"— (Isaiah 61:1), who has the very sacred personal name of the Lord God because He is God and has all of His divine attributes.

What Did Jesus Tell Us?

When we look to the New Testament we find that Jesus taught us even more about the wonderful Spirit of God. In the Gospels we read of the Holy Spirit's presence even before Jesus was born. In Luke 1:35 Mary is told by an angel that the Holy Spirit will come upon her and the power of the Most High will overshadow her. As Jesus began His earthly ministry, He went to John to be baptized and the Spirit of God descended upon Him like a dove (Matthew 3:13-17). This is where God declared, "This is my Son, whom I love; with him I am well pleased." Soon after His baptism, Jesus was led by the Spirit out to the wilderness to be tempted by the devil (Matthew 4:1).

Jesus spoke often about the Spirit. He wanted His disciples to know that they would not be left alone on this earth, so as He was getting ready to face the cross, He told them about the Advocate who would come. The word *advocate* comes from the Greek word *paraklesis*, meaning "to come alongside someone." In a court of law, it refers to one who comes and stands by your side like a lawyer interceding for his client. The noun can be also translated as "consolation, encouragement, or comfort." Jesus promised that the Father would send "the Advocate," a helper and comforter, one who would intercede for us before the Father. This same word is used to describe Jesus in 1 John 2:1 and the Father in 2 Corinthians 1:3—another beautiful reminder of the Triune God, each of whose Persons has the same characteristics.

Let's look specifically at what Jesus said about the Spirit's coming to the disciples in John 15:26: "When the Advocate comes, whom I will send to you from the Father—the Spirit of truth who goes out from the Father—he will testify about me." Jesus went on to warn them that they would face persecution after He was gone, but He reassured them they would not be alone. In John 16:4-15 we read that Jesus said it was actually good for Him to go, otherwise the Advocate would not come! Jesus wanted His disciples to know how wonderful this gift of the Holy Spirit would be.

Here are a few more descriptions Jesus gave of the Holy Spirit's work:

- He will prove the world to be in the wrong about sin and righteousness and judgment.
- He will guide you into all the truth.

- He will not speak on His own; He will speak only what He hears.

- He will tell you what is yet to come.

- He will glorify Me (Jesus).

After Jesus' death and resurrection, He appeared to His disciples numerous times. Just before He ascended to heaven, He gave them a command, "Do not leave Jerusalem, but wait for the gift my Father promised, which you have heard me speak about. For John baptized with water, but in a few days you will be baptized with the Holy Spirit." He went on to tell them, "You will receive power when the Holy Spirit comes on you; and you will be my witnesses in Jerusalem, and in all Judea and Samaria, and to the ends of the earth" (Acts 1:4-5,8).

Soon after Jesus spoke these words, the disciples and followers of Christ experienced their fulfillment. In Acts 2 we read about the coming of the Holy Spirit at Pentecost. There was a sound like a mighty rushing wind, and divided tongues as of fire appeared to them and rested on each of them. They were all filled with the Holy Spirit and began to speak in other languages as He gave them utterance. Observers thought they were drunk, but Peter stood up to clarify the situation and went on to preach a powerful sermon proclaiming the good news about Jesus. You can read his speech in Acts 2:14-41. The Bible tells us that 3000 people were added to the number of believers that day! How could an uneducated fisherman like Peter preach such a powerful message? Only by the power of the Spirit! How could 3000 people come to faith in Christ? Only by the Spirit drawing them to Himself!

Transformation

The Holy Spirit not only brings us to Christ, but He completely transforms us. The Bible says that when we come to Christ we become new creatures altogether. The Spirit actually regenerates us—we are no longer the same person we once were. Before faith in Christ, we were dead spiritually, but God's Spirit brings life. Author J.I. Packer describes it this way:

Regeneration is the spiritual change wrought in the heart of man by the Holy Spirit in which his/her inherently sinful nature is changed so that he/she can respond to God in Faith, and live in accordance with His Will (Matthew 19:28; John 3:3,5,7; Titus 3:5). It extends to the whole nature of man, altering his governing disposition, illuminating his mind, freeing his will, and renewing his nature.[2]

Isn't that fantastic? We are no longer the same person after we come to Christ. We are changed by His Spirit as He draws us to God and begins to do a good work in us, which He will carry on to completion until the day of Christ Jesus (Philippians 1:6). Packer goes on to explain, "Regeneration, or new birth, is an inner re-creating of fallen human nature by the gracious sovereign action of the Holy Spirit (John 3:5-8)."[3] The apostle John wrote, "This is how we know that we live in him and he in us: He has given us of his Spirit" (1 John 4:13). Just as a man gives a woman an engagement ring to say, "She is mine; she is my betrothed," so Jesus gave us the Holy Spirit as a seal, binding us together with Him and as evidence that we belong to Him. We are sealed to the day of redemption. The Bible goes on to tell us more about the work of the Spirit:

- *He reminds us that we are God's children.* "The Spirit you received does not make you slaves, so that you live in fear again; rather, the Spirit you received brought about your adoption to sonship. And by him we cry, 'Abba, Father.' The Spirit himself testifies with our spirit that we are God's children" (Romans 8:15-16). What a glorious revelation! We are no longer slaves; we are God's children, His heirs. It's the Spirit's job to testify with our spirit that we are His children. This fact alone should transform the way we view our lives. We can live with confidence knowing that our loving Father will always care for us. He does not treat us with animosity like a cruel taskmaster—no, the Spirit testifies that we are His beloved children.

- *He intercedes for us.* "The Spirit helps us in our weakness. We do not know what we ought to pray for, but the Spirit himself intercedes for us through wordless groans. And he who searches our hearts knows the mind of the Spirit, because the

Spirit intercedes for God's people in accordance with the will of God" (Romans 8:26-27).

- *He gives life.* "If Christ is in you, then even though your body is subject to death because of sin, the Spirit gives life because of righteousness" (Romans 8:10).

- *He is greater than the one who is in the world (Satan).* "You, dear children, are from God and have overcome them [those who belong to the world], because the one who is in you is greater than the one who is in the world" (1 John 4:4).

- *He teaches us the truth.* "You have an anointing from the Holy One, and all of you know the truth…I am writing these things to you about those who are trying to lead you astray. As for you, the anointing you received from him remains in you, and you do not need anyone to teach you. But as his anointing teaches you about all things and as that anointing is real, not counterfeit—just as it has taught you, remain in him" (1 John 2:20,26-27).

- *He leads us away from sin.* "Walk by the Spirit, and you will not gratify the desires of the flesh. For the flesh desires what is contrary to the Spirit, and the Spirit what is contrary to the flesh. They are in conflict with each other, so that you are not to do whatever you want. But if you are led by the Spirit, you are not under the law" (Galatians 5:16-18).

- *He helps us know Jesus better.* "I keep asking that the God of our Lord Jesus Christ, the glorious Father, may give you the Spirit of wisdom and revelation, so that you may know him better" (Ephesians 1:17).

- *He dwells in our hearts.* "Because you are his sons, God sent the Spirit of his Son into our hearts, the Spirit who calls out, 'Abba, Father.' So you are no longer a slave, but God's child; and since you are his child, God has made you also an heir" (Galatians 4:6).

- *He convicts the world of sin.* "When he [the Advocate] comes, he will prove the world to be in the wrong about sin and righteousness and judgment" (John 16:8).

- *He gives us courage.* "The Spirit God gave us does not make us timid, but gives us power, love and self-discipline" (2 Timothy 1:7). The same disciples who scattered when Christ went to trial stood boldly after the Holy Spirit's coming, facing persecution and death. Only His presence can give such strength, courage, and boldness.

- *He can be grieved.* "Do not grieve the Holy Spirit of God, with whom you were sealed for the day of redemption" (Ephesians 4:30).

- *His qualities are positive and useful for building up the body of Christ.* "The fruit of the Spirit is love, joy, peace, forbearance, kindness, goodness, faithfulness, gentleness and self-control" (Galatians 5:22-23).

The evidence of the Spirit's presence in our lives is love. Love is the hallmark, the signature of God's Spirit. John wrote, "God is love. Whoever lives in love lives in God and God in them" (1 John 4:16). John also wrote, "No one has ever seen God; but if we love one another, God lives in us and his love is made complete in us" (1 John 4:12).

May the world see this kind of love pouring through our lives as a result of His Spirit within us. Think of how others would be drawn to Christ if they saw us do everything in a spirit of love. If you are having trouble loving others, ask His Spirit who lives in you to love through you. Ask Him to gently convict you of any bitterness or unforgiveness you need to turn from; then, in His power, move forward in love. God is love, and if His Spirit is living in you, He is able to love through you in a big way, a supernatural way.

His Leading

Recently a friend of mine watched the Disney remake of the movie *The Miracle Worker*. As she was watching, she had an "aha" moment about the analogy this story gives us of being led by the Spirit. Think about young Helen Keller, blind and deaf, not able to understand the world around her.

Yet her loving father provided a teacher (Annie Sullivan) to teach her and guide her. One day at the well, Annie spelled the word *water* in Helen's hand. Helen had been rebellious and had fought against her teacher, but something changed that day—she got it. She had a breakthrough moment and surrendered her will to that of her teacher. She allowed her to lead her, teach her, and guide her.

You know Helen Keller's story. She went on to do amazing things. She graduated from Radcliffe College, spoke across the nation and around the world, and inspired millions of people, as she still does to this day. Although *she* couldn't see and hear, *her teacher* could. Her teacher became her ears and eyes; all Helen needed to do was surrender and listen. May we be like Helen, allowing our Great Teacher, the Holy Spirit, to guide us and direct us.

Sadly, we are often like Helen was before she had her "aha" moment at the well. We want to go our own way and live our own life, not listening to the loving teacher our Father has provided for us. But what a difference a surrendered heart makes! Oh, the joy of loving and trusting our Great Helper, our Advocate, our Comforter and Teacher! Are you willing to surrender and trust His faithful leading? Romans 8:14 reminds us that those who are led by the Spirit of God are the children of God. If you struggle with the idea of surrender, just remember that He will help you even to surrender. Lean into His loving arms, and He will gently lead you to a place of surrender. It is God who works in us both to will and to work for His good pleasure.

As I bring this chapter to a close, my only regret is that there is not enough room to write all that the Bible teaches us about the Holy Spirit and the gifts that He gives us. So I encourage you to explore and study the Scriptures on your own. Remember you have the Holy Spirit within you to lead you and guide you and teach you about Himself. Ask Him to show you more about His presence in you and to open your eyes and heart to the immeasurable power He brings to your life. I encourage you to read the book of Acts for yourself and take note of all the ways the gifts of the Spirit are evidenced in the lives of the early believers. Seek to know more about His mighty power; He will reveal Himself to those who seek Him.

Digging Deeper

Read 1 Corinthians 12 and Romans 12 and write in your journal what you learn about spiritual gifts and how they can and should be used to build up the body of Christ.

DISCUSS

1. How have you sensed the presence of God's Spirit in your own life?

2. In what areas of your life are you trying to function on your own strength and power? In what areas are you surrendering to the leading of the Holy Spirit?

3. How does it make you feel loved, knowing that your heavenly Father has given you His Spirit?

HELPFUL RESOURCES

- *Understanding Spiritual Gifts* by Kay Arthur
- *What's So Spiritual About Your Gifts?* by Henry Blackaby
- *The Spirit of Christ* by Andrew Murray
- *Absolute Surrender* by Andrew Murray
- *They Found the Secret* by V. Raymond Edmund

Seven Loving Words

The one who gets wisdom loves life;
the one who cherishes understanding will soon prosper.

PROVERBS 19:8

Love is something more stern and splendid than mere kindness …
If God is Love, He is, by definition,
something more than mere kindness …
He has paid us the interable compliment of loving us,
in the deepest, most tragic, most memorable sense.

C.S. LEWIS

*W*hen I was in seventh grade, our French class was assigned to read *The Little Prince* by French author Antoine de Saint-Exupery. It's a simple little novella and the assignment appeared to be easy. There was only one challenge—we were required to read it *en français* (in French)! *Le Petit Prince* was slightly more challenging to read. In fact I remember keeping my French dictionary close at hand as I stumbled through the entire work. Believe me, I wanted to give up at the turn of every page. My knowledge of French was meager, and as a little seventh-grader, I couldn't quite grasp the philosophical implications of the prince (who was from an asteroid, no less) and the unique tales he told to a stranded pilot in the middle of a desert.

Are you getting the picture of why I had trouble understanding the book? Have you ever struggled to read a book that seemed to make no sense at all? Perhaps at times you have felt that way about the Bible. Words, concepts, or phrases may have seemed completely foreign to you and you simply felt like giving up. When we encounter a book that is not easy to read, we tend to want to push it aside and read something easier. Often I hear people say that they don't read the Bible because they can't understand it. So if it is meant for us to read and apply to our lives, why does it seem difficult to understand? Is God trying to confuse us? Certainly not! God loves us and wants us to understand His truth, that's why He gave us the Holy Spirit to lead us and give us understanding.

One of the reasons some of the Bible may seem hard to understand is that there are both time and cultural differences. The cultures in which its writers lived is much different than the culture in which we live. Words that were typically used thousands of years ago may seem a little foreign to us today. That doesn't mean that the Bible is not relevant, it just means that we may need to enrich our understanding of the terms and words that are used.

Words that may initially seem strange to us can actually become beautiful and life-giving. In this chapter I want to unveil the beauty of seven words that may seem hard to understand. My hope is that you will come to see these terms as some of the most loving words in the Bible, because each one allows us to understand God's grace-filled love toward us.

1. Repentance

In Matthew 4:17 we read, "From that time on Jesus began to preach, 'Repent, for the kingdom of heaven has come near.'" Jesus began His earthly ministry with a call to repentance, so it is important for us to understand how the word should be applied to our own lives. The word *repentance* (Greek *metanoia*) literally means "change of mind." Repentance is more than just regret or feeling sorry about what we did; it means turning from sin and changing the way we think. It refers to a new outlook; turning from old ways and seeing things in accordance with God's will. The parable of the Prodigal Son is a beautiful example of repentance, in which we find the son who left home and squandered his inheritance, returning to his father with a humbled heart and ready to change his ways.

In Acts 11:18 we read, "Even to Gentiles God has granted repentance that leads to life." God gives us the ability to repent, to see things in a new way. Repentance not only refers to turning away from sin, but it also encompasses a turning to God in faith. Jesus said, "I have not come to call the righteous, but sinners to repentance" (Luke 5:32). He came to call us to a change of mind, turning our minds from the direction of sin and turning toward the love of God. Each of us must come to a point of recognizing our own sinfulness and turning to God for help.

2. Atonement

The word *atonement* is primarily used in the Old Testament. The Hebrew word is *kaphar*, meaning "to cover, placate, or cancel." It was a technical term in Israel's sacrificial rituals. In some ways, the word *atonement* can be likened to a material transaction or ransom. In Exodus 32:30, Moses ascended to the mountain a third time to make atonement for the people's sin. The word is most often used in regard to the priests and the ritual sacrifices. In Exodus, Leviticus, and Numbers we find the priests smearing the blood of the sacrificed animal on the altar during the sin offering. The most important place we see the word is in "Day of Atonement." Only on this day could the high priest enter the holy of holies in the temple on behalf the Israelites and make atonement for them before God.

So why is atonement important to you and me, especially if it is an Old Testament word? The need for atonement is a central theme to the Bible. Our sins must be atoned for in order for us to come before a righteous God. Isn't it wonderful to know that God seeks to reconcile sinful people to Himself? The fact that a holy and righteous God would make a way for sinners to be forgiven is a beautiful truth in and of itself.

3. Propitiation

Closely related to atonement is the word *propitiation*—not a word we use every day, but it is a powerfully potent word nonetheless. It's interesting to examine the word *propitiation* in the Greek. *Hilasterion* means "to turn aside wrath or appease," and is closely related to the adjective *hilaron*, which means "cheerful." Yes, it is where we get the English word *hilarious*. Doesn't that make sense? When we have done something wrong and yet our penalty has been paid, we feel a cheerful sense of relief. We experience a sense of joy and gratitude when the wrath or punishment we deserve has been appeased or set aside completely. We find the word *propitiation* used several times in the New Testament (Romans 3:25; Hebrews 9:5; 1 John 2:2; 4:10). Propitiation is an expression of God's love for us. John wrote,

"In this is love, not that we have loved God but that he loved us and sent his Son to be the propitiation for our sins" (1 John 4:10 ESV).

The concept of mercy and propitiation go hand in hand. In Romans we see that Jesus' blood is the propitiation for our sins.

> There is no distinction: for all have sinned and fall short of the glory of God, and are justified by his grace as a gift, through the redemption that is in Christ Jesus, whom God put forward as a *propitiation* by his blood, to be received by faith. This was to show God's righteousness, because in his divine forbearance he had passed over former sins (Romans 3:23-25 ESV).

Often the word *hilasterion* is translated as "atoning," but propitiation heavily leans on mercy and reminds us of God's mercy toward each one of us as sinners. Perhaps you are familiar with the Sinners Prayer found in Luke 18:13: "God, be merciful to me a sinner." Actually it should be translated, "God, be propitious to me a sinner." Propitiation reminds us that although we have sinned, God is merciful toward us because of the blood of Christ. We are the recipients of His gracious mercy. Now doesn't that make you cheerful?

4. Justification

The word *justification* (Greek, *dikaiosis*) means "to be declared righteous or receive a complete acquittal." God declares a sinner to be justified (righteous) at the moment she despairs of her own unrighteousness and clings to the righteousness of Christ. It is a declaration by God that occurs at the beginning of the Christian life, not at the end. Believers' justification is not partial, and it is not merited by their own works. Our justification is merited by Christ alone. We are justified through faith based on what Christ did for us on the cross. Paul wrote about this marvelous justification in his letter to the Romans:

> Just as one trespass resulted in condemnation for all people, so also one righteous act resulted in *justification* and life for all people. For just as through the disobedience of the one man the many were made sinners, so also through the

obedience of the one man the many will be made righteous (Romans 5:18-19).

To be clear, justification is not a process but rather a declaration—God's declaration on the basis of Christ's righteousness. I love what John Stott wrote about justification: "The real reason why the doctrine of justification by grace alone through faith alone is unpopular is that it is grievously wounding to our pride."[1] Yes, deep inside we pridefully want to think that we have earned our way into God's good graces, by something we have done. Justification is a freeing reminder that our salvation is not dependent on our works, but on His work.

> When the goodness and loving kindness of God our Savior appeared, he saved us, not because of works done by us in righteousness, but according to his own mercy, by the washing of regeneration and renewal of the Holy Spirit, whom he poured out on us richly through Jesus Christ our Savior, so that being *justified* by his grace we might become heirs according to the hope of eternal life (Titus 3:4-7).

5. Grace

Grace is a short word with a big meaning. Often we use the word to refer to gracious behavior or graceful dancing or even saying a mealtime prayer, but grace represents the very reason for our joy as believers. In the Old Testament, we find the Hebrew word *chen*, meaning "kindness or favor." It was first used in Genesis (6:8), "But Noah found grace in the eyes of the LORD." In the book of Ruth, I especially love how we find the word *chen* used by Ruth as she speaks to Boaz (her kinsman redeemer), "Why have I found favor in your eyes that you should take notice of me, when I am a foreigner?" What a beautiful picture of God's grace toward us. Why should we as sinners find favor in the eyes of an all-holy God? One word: *grace*.

In the New Testament the Hebrew word for grace is *charis*, referring to God's unmerited favor. There are many spiritual implications from this one mighty word—and to truly grasp its full meaning is to embrace the essence of Christianity. Grace is not about us; it is all about God.

B.B. Warfield said, "Grace is free sovereign favor to the ill-deserving." Free is a very important part of understanding God's grace. Other religions are not based on grace, they are based on working to please and make amends with their god or gods. The Christian faith is different. It is not based on our merit, but on God's goodness, love, and kindness toward us.

Although grace is free, it is not cheap. We must never take the grace of God for granted, but rather live in thankful obedience as a result of understanding this amazing and unmerited favor God has bestowed on us. A.W. Tozer wrote: "Grace is the good pleasure of God that inclines him to bestow benefits on the undeserving." Perhaps you have seen the acronym for GRACE: God's Riches at Christ's Expense, which is a great reminder of the high cost of God's grace. John MacArthur took it further by saying, "Grace is not merely unmerited favor; it is favor bestowed on sinners who deserve wrath. Showing kindness to a stranger is 'unmerited favor'; doing good to one's enemies is more the spirit of grace."

Romans 5:1-2,6-8 describes our reason to rejoice:

> Since we have been justified through faith, we have peace with God through our Lord Jesus Christ, through whom we have gained access by faith into this grace in which we now stand. And we boast in the hope of the glory of God...
>
> You see, at just the right time, when we were still powerless, Christ died for the ungodly. Very rarely will anyone die for a righteous person, though for a good person someone might possibly dare to die. But God demonstrates his own love for us in this: While we were still sinners, Christ died for us.

For me personally, I find myself continually thankful and joyful because of this very passage describing God's grace. "Amazing Grace, how sweet the sound that saved a wretch like me. I once was lost but now am found, was blind, but now I see!" Because of His grace I desire to walk in fellowship with Him. Because of His grace, I am compelled to show grace to the people around me. What about you? How does God's grace affect your daily life?

6. Sanctification

The actual word *sanctification* is used only five times in the New Testament, but variations of the word (*sanctify, sanctified, sanctifies*) can be found over 130 times in both the Old and New Testament. In Greek, the word for *sanctification* is *hagiasmos*, meaning "a purifier, to make holy." This is where we get the word *saints* (*hagioi*), meaning holy ones. Jesus prayed for believers saying, "Sanctify them in the truth; your word is truth...for their sake I consecrate myself, that they also may be sanctified in truth" (John 17:17). God's word of truth sanctifies us, as well as the Spirit of truth.

The Westminster Shorter Catechism (Q. 35) defines sanctification as "the work of God's free grace, whereby we are renewed in the whole man after the image of God, and are enabled more and more to die unto sin, and live unto righteousness." Nathan W. Bingham adds this concerning sanctification:

> It is a continuing change worked by God in us, freeing us from sinful habits and forming in us Christlike affections, dispositions, and virtues. It does not mean that sin is instantly eradicated, but it is also more than a counteraction, in which sin is merely restrained or repressed without being progressively destroyed. Sanctification is a real transformation, not just the appearance of one.[2]

Isn't it wonderful to know that God not only calls us to holiness, but He does the work within us through the power of His Spirit? When we open our hearts in faith to God, His Holy Spirit begins to do a work in our lives leading us to be more Christlike in our words and actions. First Thessalonians 4:7 tells us, "God has not called us for impurity, but in holiness (*hagiasmos*)." Thankfully, sanctification is an ongoing process. It is dependent on God's continual work in the lives of believers, and also consists of the believers' continual struggle against sin. Putting it succinctly, sanctification is human effort, yet dependent on God's work within us.

7. Gospel

The word *gospel* is a New Testament term repeated in over a hundred verses. The Greek word *euangelion* (the root from which we get the word *evangelical*) means the "good news" of the kingdom of God. In the Gospel of Mark, we read, "Jesus came into Galilee, proclaiming the gospel of God, and saying, 'The time is fulfilled, and the kingdom of God is at hand; repent and believe in the gospel'" (Mark 1:14-15 ESV). Jesus proclaimed the good news of the kingdom of God.

So what is the "good news"? The good news is wrapped up in the person of Jesus Christ. The good news is that God loves us and reconciled us to Himself through Jesus Christ. The good news is that we are justified through faith in Him, not by our own righteousness but by His. The good news is that He has given us His Holy Spirit, to regenerate us, sanctify us, and empower us to live with strength and victory. The good news is that God will never leave us or forsake us. The good news is that we have the promise of eternal life through Jesus. The good news is that God is our Abba (daddy) Father and we are His children, heirs of God and co-heirs with Christ. The good news is that God is continually at work in our lives; He began a good work in us and will carry it on to completion until the day of Christ Jesus. We are no longer slaves to sin, for we have been rescued from the dominion of darkness and brought into the kingdom of the Son who God the Father loves—that's good news! Recently I heard it put this way: "The gospel is not good advice on how we can work our way to heaven—rather it is good news that God offered His Son, so that all who believe may be saved by His grace."

I'm reminded of what Harry Foster wrote: "The gospel is the gospel of a happy God, because he now has an ever-growing family of those who by faith share the perfect life of his perfect son."[3] As Christians we have received great and precious promises. Funny thing, when the word *gospel* has been translated into different languages the translators have used phrases such as "information that causes one joy" or "words that bring smiles" or "news that makes one happy." Remember what the angels declared to the shepherds on the night of Jesus' birth? They said they were bringing "good tidings of great joy." They were announcing the gospel! When we recognize all that God has done for us and continues to do through us, we can't help but be filled with joy. May the joy of the gospel overflow in our lives as we live each day for His kingdom. Let us be bearers of good news!

Digging Deeper

Read Romans 8 and record in your journal all the blessings and benefits of being a follower of Christ.

DISCUSS

1. Which words in this chapter helped you understand the love of the Father for you?

2. When we get good news we tend to want to share it. How does the gospel of Christ impact your life and how are you sharing it with others?

3. Why do you think the concept of grace is considered the foundation of the Christian faith?

HELPFUL RESOURCES

- *The Gospel According to the Apostles* by John MacArthur
- *The Grace of God* by Andy Stanley
- *Transforming Grace* by Jerry Bridges
- *Scandalous Freedom* by Steve Brown
- *Truths That Transform, Christian Doctrines for Your Life Today* by D. James Kennedy

Part Three

Living the Bible

~

Do not merely listen to the word,
and so deceive yourselves.
Do what it says.

James 1:22

No Christian is where he ought to be spiritually
until the beauty of the Lord Jesus Christ
is being reproduced in daily Christian life.

A.W. Tozer

The Bible is a living document; it is unlike any other book you might have on your shelves. As you come to know and love it, it inspires a deeper calling within you. God means the truths of His Word to transform you, to change you, and to move you to action. When you immerse yourself in Scripture, the principles in the Word—indeed, God's very life—begin to overflow from your heart and touch the lives of others.

My hope is that the following chapters will give each of us a little nudge and lift us out of our comfy chairs and into the world, which so desperately needs to experience God's love. These chapters are intended to move us to make an impact in the world, to engage with the culture, to pray fervently, to worship joyfully, and to live as His loving body, the church.

We don't want to simply take in the words of the Bible and keep them for ourselves. We want to live them out using the unique gifts God has given us. What is He urging you to do through His Word? May His Spirit use His very words to move you to action and reach out and touch the lives of others with His love and compassion.

11

How to Have Zero Impact in the World

I am the vine; you are the branches. If you remain in me and I in you, you will bear much fruit; apart from me you can do nothing.

JOHN 15:5

*Holiness is not the laborious acquisition
of virtue from without,
but the expression of the Christ-life from within.*

J.W.C. WAND

Now I know that you may be surprised by the seemingly negative title of this chapter, especially coming from the "Positive Lady." You would expect to see a chapter on "How to Live a Meaningful Life" or "Seven Secrets to Making a Difference in the World." Not a chapter that shares how to have absolutely no impact in this world. To my credit, I didn't come up with the idea on my own—it was really Paul's idea. In his first letter to the Corinthians he gave us one easy way to make no difference at all in this world. Are you curious what he wrote? Here it is:

> If I speak in the tongues of men or of angels, but do not have love, I am only a resounding gong or a clanging cymbal. If I have the gift of prophecy and can fathom all mysteries and all knowledge, and if I have a faith that can move mountains, but do not have love, I am nothing. If I give all I possess to the poor and give over my body to hardship that I may boast, but do not have love, I gain nothing (1 Corinthians 13:1-3).

In the first sentence of this passage, Paul mentions a resounding gong.

Now, we don't use gongs on a regular basis in our culture, but I think that obnoxious blow horns could be a strong comparison. Several years ago my husband and I attended our daughter's graduation from Texas A&M. Now in Texas we do things big and that includes class sizes and graduations. There were thousands graduating from just one school within the university. Knowing we would be there for hours, my husband and I brought books to read while we waited for our daughter's name to be called. We were settled comfortably in our stadium chairs enjoying an opportunity to sit and read for a while, when our relaxed setting was shockingly defiled by the sound of a blow horn. Not only did the people behind us blow the horn for their own darling graduate, but apparently they knew three-quarters of the graduating class!

If you have ever been in a similar situation you know the unnerving sound that comes from these annoying horns. So let's think about this blow horn in context with our passage. If I speak with the tongues of men and of angels, but do not have love, I'm like that blow horn. Maybe you are not a speaker or a preacher, so this doesn't mean as much to you. But consider what you are gifted at doing. Maybe it is cooking or making business deals or selling houses or raising kids—if it is done without love, you're like that blow horn. He goes on to say if I use the gifts God has given me, but do not have love, I am nothing. Finally Paul says, even if I sacrificially give away all my stuff so that I look really great, but do not have love, I gain nothing.

Gaining nothing is what I call "zero impact." We may think we have done a lot of great things, but if it is not done with love, it has zero impact. If I have great faith and can spout off a gazillion Bible verses from memory (as a result of chapter 5 in this book of course), but my life is not marked by love, I gain nothing. If I feed the homeless and sacrifice my time to volunteer at the local crisis pregnancy center, but am hateful or gossipy or unkind, I am not making an impact for His kingdom.

His Help to Love

Now, I'm fairly certain that if you are reading this book you do want to have a positive impact in the world. On the upside, Paul doesn't just leave us hanging without hope, he actually goes on to list the secret ingredients that give our lives mega-impact. He gives us a description of love. Here's how he continued:

> Love is patient, love is kind. It does not envy, it does not boast, it is not proud. It does not dishonor others, it is not self-seeking, it is not easily angered, it keeps no record of wrongs. Love does not delight in evil but rejoices with the truth. It always protects, always trusts, always hopes, always perseveres. Love never fails (1 Corinthians 13:4-8).

Think about the influential power these actions have in making a difference in the lives of the people around us. Talk about having a positive impact! This kind of love open doors, builds into lives, and strengthens hearts. The love described here is culture-changing, eye-opening, and life transforming! It is beyond human love; it is supernatural. I want this kind of love to be evident in my life, don't you? But I can't exactly love like this in my own power and strength. Ultimately this description of love is a description of God Himself, because God is love. John the beloved disciple wrote,

> Dear friends, let us love one another, for love comes from God. Everyone who loves has been born of God and knows God. Whoever does not love does not know God, because God is love. This is how God showed his love among us: He sent his one and only Son into the world that we might live through him. This is love: not that we loved God, but that he loved us and sent his Son as an atoning sacrifice for our sins. Dear friends, since God so loved us, we also ought to love one another. No one has ever seen God; but if we love one another, God lives in us and his love is made complete in us (1 John 4:7-12).

God not only showed us what love looked like by sending His Son, Jesus, He also gave us His Spirit to love the world through us. We may struggle to love with this divine kind of sacrificial love, but we can ask God, whose very essence is love, to pour His love through us. Each day as we make our plan of what we need to accomplish, let us ask God to love through us. In every deed and action, every errand and responsibility, may His supernatural love be evident in all we say and do. Early in the morning, I make it a practice to write out my daily schedule. Then once I have it all figured out, I take a pink highlighter and write the word *love* over it all. It serves as a visual reminder to me that if I am doing a plethora of great activities, but do not show love to the people around me, it is all worthless. Net zero.

Letting Him Do the Work

Just as we can't love in our own strength and power, we can't live obedient and meaningful lives in our own strength and power either. Recently a friend said to me, "God didn't design us to work for Him. Rather He designed us in a way for Him to work through us." It's easy to think that God's work depends on us, when in reality it completely depends on Him. He wants to flow through us. Just before Jesus was going to the cross, He encouraged His disciples saying, "Very truly I tell you, whoever believes in me will do the works I have been doing, and they will do even greater things than these, because I am going to the Father. And I will do whatever you ask in my name, so that the Father may be glorified in the Son. You may ask me for anything in my name, and I will do it" (John 14:12-14).

Now that is one heaping dose of encouragement! He told the disciples that they would do greater works than what they had seen Jesus do. And they did! Check out the section about miracles found in the back of this book. But the important thing I want you to notice are the words, "*I* will do it." He said, "I will do whatever you ask." He will do great works through us. What is our job? It is to ask. What if the greatest work we do is on our knees, asking, seeking, knocking? Have you ever considered the most important "doing" you can do is to pray? Then as God leads, you can go and do wonderful things, but it is Him doing it, not you. He gets the glory.

Have you ever seen a little toddler screaming, "I can do it myself"? And usually they can't, but they sure want to try! We are never so much like a two-year-old as when we try to accomplish good works and great things on our own. Jesus said, "I am the vine; you are the branches. If you remain in me and I in you, you will bear much fruit; apart from me you can do nothing" (John 15:5). There's that word again: "nothing." Another net zero. When we try to accomplish kingdom work apart from Him we can do nothing. On the contrary, if we abide in Him and He in us, we will bear much fruit.

One of the deepest needs we have as women is to feel like we are doing something meaningful. If we are abiding in Him, then we will be fruitful, no matter what we are doing. Abiding in Him makes working at a coffee shop fruitful work. Abiding in Him makes taking care of our kids fruitful work. Abiding in Him makes working at a large corporation fruitful work. How wonderful that God wants to work through us to impact the world. He wants us to fellowship (partner) with Him to do the work He has purposed us and created us to do. Is it hard work to "abide in Christ"? Actually, *abiding* means "to dwell, remain, or live" in Him. That's not hard work. It's a matter of enjoying His presence in our life and surrendering our will to His leading.

Out of the Saltshaker

When I was in college I read a book by Rebecca Manley Pippert called *Out of the Saltshaker and into the World*. It's one of those books that has stuck in my mind for years because the message is truthful and powerful. As Christians, our tendency is to stick together, going to church, attending Bible studies, and enjoying fellowships and gatherings. Why? Because that's where our like-minded friends are and where we feel safe. There is nothing wrong with enjoying these activities, but Jesus told us to be salt and light in this world. How can we salt or flavor this world if we spend all our time in the saltshaker?

In His Sermon on the Mount, Jesus identified His followers as both "salt and light." I love the fact that He tells us we are salt. Salt was a valuable commodity in His day. It was used to preserve meat, and it is also essential for our physical bodies to function. It flavors our food and makes us thirsty for more. Yet if salt remains in the saltshaker, it is useless. Could it be that we as Christ's followers have become too comfortable in the saltshaker?

We go to Bible studies at church, we gain knowledge, and we enjoy fellowship, but are we putting into practice the very words that we are studying? Is there a disconnect between knowing what the Bible has to say and actually putting His words into practice, flavoring the world with His love and grace and the gospel?

Recently, I heard about a life group in Houston that wanted to do more than simply meet every week and feed themselves spiritually, so they decided to begin reaching out to others twice a month. One meeting per month was dedicated to serving at a shelter for battered women. Another night was designated as a game night in order to reach out to the unchurched. Now that's being salt! Out of the saltshaker and into the world. Let's courageously jump in! Pastor Michael Catt says, "People of courage make a way where there is no way. Instead of cowering to the pressures of this culture, Christians need to become a force for positive peer pressure. We need to break out of the box...Boxes are designed for storage, not saints."[1]

Zero vs. Powerful

Let's sum up what we learned in this chapter. If we want to have zero impact in this world, there are three surefire ways to do it:

1. Do a lot of good things, but do them without love.
2. Do great and wonderful things in your own strength and power.
3. Stay safe. Don't engage with the culture—just do a lot of church stuff.

I know that's not your heart. You *do* want to have an impact on the culture. So if you want to be a vessel used by Him, then:

1. Allow His love to flow through you in everything you do and say.
2. Ask, seek, and knock. Abide with Him each day; don't try to do good works on your own.
3. Engage with the culture. Be salt and light in this world.

Allow me to share an illustration that God so lovingly showed me. One day while I was at our little cottage in Austin, Texas, where I go to write, I was sitting out on the back porch enjoying some time of prayer. I saw a hummingbird flit by, busy with activity, going from one flower to another. I was struck by the lovely sight of this tiny little bird, and so I asked the Lord if He wanted me to be like that hummingbird, busily fly-ing around and working hard doing its job. In a still small voice, I sensed God speak into my mind, "No, Karol—I do not want you to be like that hummingbird."

I then asked the Lord to show me something in nature that my life was supposed to be like. I know this may sound strange, but in the still-ness of my quiet time with the Lord, the thought came to my mind that I was to be a like a riverbed. What? A riverbed? That's not fun or glamorous. It just lies there and the water flows over it. The thought and impression was so strong on my mind that I decided to walk down to the riverbed close to our cottage.

Just so you know, at that time in Austin, the river was completely dried up. They had experienced drought in the area for years. When I went down to where the river was supposed to be, the docks were all lean-ing on their sides and boats were on dry ground. The riverbed even had plants growing in it. As I looked at the plants I thought to myself that they looked kind of pretty there, but the Lord reminded me that the riverbed wasn't meant for plants, it was meant for water. I realized that just like that riverbed, there were some weeds that I had allowed to grow in my life that needed to be rooted out. Things like unforgiveness and jealousy.

Then I looked at the riverbed and imagined what it would look like if it was filled with water. Oh, I pictured the boats and the docks being use-ful and purposeful once again. It occurred to me that if I tried to lift up those boats and docks in my own strength, I couldn't do it, but if the water filled the riverbed, it would lift up the boats and docks with its strength. I thought to myself, *It would take a miracle to have enough rain to fill this riverbed again.* That's when it hit me, making an impact or a difference in the lives of others is not by my strength and power, it is by His. It is a miracle. He can do far more than I ask or imagine as He pours His Spirit through me.

Interestingly, as I came back to my cottage and returned to my writing project, the very passage I came to was John 7. Here's what it said, "On the last and greatest day of the festival, Jesus stood and said in a loud voice, 'Let anyone who is thirsty come to me and drink. Whoever believes in me, as Scripture has said, rivers of living water will flow from within them.' By this he meant the Spirit, whom those who believed in him were later to receive. Up to that time the Spirit had not been given, since Jesus had not yet been glorified."

Can you believe it? What an amazing confirmation! The lesson I learned that day and have continued to ponder each day is the message of surrender. As I lay down my life, like a riverbed, and surrender my will to His, the Holy Spirit does the work as He flows through me and lifts up the lives of others. It's not about me, but about His Spirit pouring through me. My friends, if we want to have an impact in this world it begins with daily surrender, seeking His agenda, and walking with Him. Without Him, we can do nothing—zero impact!

Digging Deeper

Read Titus 3 and record in your journal everything you learn personally about living biblically in our culture today.

DISCUSS

1. Why do you think some Christians do or say things in an unloving way?

2. Describe a time that you knew God was flowing through you as you reached out to others.

3. Why is it important for Christians to be salt and light in our world today?

HELPFUL RESOURCES

- *Out of the Saltshaker and into the World* by Rebecca Manley Pippert
- *How Should We Then Live?* by Francis A. Schaeffer
- *How Now Shall We Live?* by Charles Colson and Nancy Pearcey

12

Fully Engaged

Religion that God our Father accepts as pure and faultless is this:
to look after orphans and widows in their distress
and to keep oneself from being polluted by the world.

JAMES 1:27

The Christians who have turned the world upside down
have been men and women with a vision in their hearts
and the Bible in their hands.

T.B. MASTON

 *L*eslie belonged to two different Bible studies, and it was starting to bother her. She wasn't bothered by what she was learning in the Bible. On the contrary, she loved studying God's Word and she also loved hanging out with all of her friends in the study groups. What bothered Leslie was the fact that she had a lot of Bible knowledge, but she wasn't using it to affect the culture. As we said in the last chapter, she was enjoying her life in the saltshaker, and she realized it was time to get out and flavor the world with His love. She decided to join our Engage Parenting Initiative and reach into the lives of moms in at-risk communities.

It wasn't easy to choose to leave one of her Bible studies, yet she knew she was doing exactly what the Word of God tells us to do—engage with the culture. Leslie didn't know all that the future held for her, but she went forward fully equipped with God's love and ready to pour it into the lives of others. The one thing I appreciate most about Leslie is that she doesn't serve with an attitude of "I'm going to go and fix people." Instead, her focus is to build relationships with the moms and help them experience the love of Jesus through her words and actions. Leslie allowed God's love to flow through her and she has had a positive impact in their lives.

As we engage with the culture and point people to the love of Christ, we must come with hearts of service, not of arrogance. Paul reminds us to do nothing out of selfish ambition or vain conceit; rather, with humility we should consider others better than ourselves. That doesn't mean that we put ourselves down; it means that we build others up through love and service. Think about the powerful effect we as Christians would have in this world if we adopted this attitude in all we say and do. Paul went on to say,

> In your relationships with one another, have the same
> mindset as Christ Jesus:
>> Who, being in very nature God,
>>> did not consider equality with God something to be
>>> used to his own advantage;
>> rather, he made himself nothing
>>> by taking the very nature of a servant,
>>> being made in human likeness.
>> And being found in appearance as a man,
>>> he humbled himself
>>> by becoming obedient to death—
>>> even death on a cross!
>> Therefore God exalted him to the highest place
>>> and gave him the name that is above every name,
>>> that at the name of Jesus every knee should bow,
>>> in heaven and on earth and under the earth,
>> and every tongue acknowledge that Jesus Christ is Lord,
>>> to the glory of God the Father (Philippians 2:5-11).

If unbelievers saw Christians who sincerely laid down their lives in love, humility, and service, I believe they would be drawn to Christ. Sadly, they often see hypocrites. They see Christians who love themselves more than they love God or others. We can be different! As women of the Word, we can engage with the culture through a heart of service. A riverbed attitude, if you will. *Lord, let us live with Christ's love and humility, let it begin with me.*

Connecting Through Conversation

One of the most important ways for us to engage with our culture is to encourage healthy conversation instead of shutting down conversations. How do we shut down dialogue? By failing to listen. When we are willing to listen to the people God puts in our path and converse back and forth, we open up the possibilities for building into the lives of others. It's easy as Christians to think it is our duty to set everyone straight and let them know where they are wrong. Jesus wasn't afraid to engage with sinners. He asked questions. He listened. He loved and did not condemn. He showed us what it looked like to engage with the culture by reaching into the lives of people who needed His love.

Paul wrote, "Whatever you do, whether in word or deed, do it all in the name of the Lord Jesus, giving thanks to God the Father through him." He went on to say, "Be wise in the way you act toward outsiders; make the most of every opportunity. Let your conversation be always full of grace, seasoned with salt, so that you may know how to answer everyone" (Colossians 4:5-6). So how do we speak the truth of God's Word, while lovingly reaching out to the culture around us? We must be both gracious and wise in what comes out of our mouths, recognizing that those who do not know Christ do not see life through the same perspective.

Theologian and philosopher Francis Schaeffer wrote, "Each generation of the church in each setting has the responsibility of communicating the gospel in understandable terms, considering the language and thought-forms of that setting."[1] Often Jesus answered a question with a question. Questions can help us get to the heart of the matter and lead people toward truth. Recently I had an e-mail dialogue with one of my readers that went something like this.

> Reader: *Do you think* _____ *is a sin?*
>
> Me: *Why do you want to know?*
>
> Reader: *I want to know if God is mad at me.*
>
> Me: *Why do you care if God is mad at you?*
>
> Reader: *I want to know if I am disobeying Him. I don't want to feel far away from Him.*
>
> Me: *If you care about what God thinks about you, then you don't need to know what I think about that sin, rather you need to know what God says about it.*

I then led her to the passage in Romans 3 that reminds us that we have *all* sinned and fallen short of God's glory. We all have a sin problem, and yet God in His loving-kindness provided the solution to our sin problem through Jesus Christ. I led her to passages in the Bible about Jesus, so that she could understand His love and mercy, as well as His righteousness and His desire for her life. You see, we need to lead people to the love of Jesus first, because without Him, picking out *this* sin or *that* sin is meaningless and unfruitful. When someone is inquiring about sin, they either sincerely want to know what God thinks about sin, or they are trying to get you to say something so that they will feel offended (and sadly this is usually the case).

The message of the Bible is simple: We all fall short of God's glory, and we all need Jesus. Our objective is to argue less and point to God more. Often our words can be misunderstood or not received in the spirit in which we give them. The most important thing we can do is to refrain from surface-level disputes and instead get to the real issue of the heart. Ask questions, listen, engage in conversation, and lovingly lead people to the core issue of Christ's love. Remember how Jesus handled the woman caught in adultery? The Pharisees brought her to Jesus wanting Him to condemn her. Jesus wisely and gently responded by pointing out the fact that all have sinned. We all need Jesus. Our job is not to cast stones at sinners; our job is to point to the gospel of salvation.

Instead of condemning, we ought to be engaging and shining the light of Christ. Our first objective is to live biblically and examine our own hearts and motives, repenting and seeking the Holy Spirit's help in living righteous lives ourselves. As we humbly reflect the love of Jesus in our words and actions, then we have the platform to lovingly share the gospel with a world that desperately needs Him. Am I willing to step out and touch the people who are different than me, just as Jesus did? It all comes down to asking ourselves, "Am I willing to take the time to engage in conversations and build relationships with those who need Christ?"

Do You Know Your Neighbor?

Jesus told us to "love our neighbor as ourselves," but how many of us really know our neighbors? Have you ever thought about the transformation that could take place if Christians reached out and loved the people that God had placed right next door? Isn't it sad that as believers we all huddle together at our churches and enjoy the fellowship with our own group, but we don't make a difference in our neighborhoods?

What if, like my friend Leslie, we decided to do one less Bible study or church activity and instead become more actively involved in the lives of the people God has put right in our path—our neighbors. What would that look like? How about inviting your neighbors over for dinner or for a cookout or to watch a game? Maybe you could meet for coffee or a meal at a local restaurant. What if you decided to start a neighborhood book study or Bible study? When I was a young mom, I felt so isolated, and I didn't know any of the other moms on my street. I was going to a large, mega Bible study at my church, but I felt God's tug that I needed to reach out to the moms on my street.

I began praying that God would give me another woman in the neighborhood who had a similar vision. Since we didn't know anyone in the neighborhood, my husband and I joined the homeowners' association and decided to get involved. We joined the dinner club and the vegetable co-op, and I started investing time with our neighbors. Through the dinner club, I met one Christian woman who had the same heart for reaching out to neighbors as I did. Together we decided to start a Bible study. We chose a book to study, then made flyers inviting our neighbors to a Bible study. We had no idea if anyone would show up, but God knew!

He brought five women from all different backgrounds and denominations. Some were familiar with the Bible, and others were curious to know more. The group grew and we became a heart sisterhood of support to one another. We experienced life together. We had baby showers, picnics, and holiday gatherings. We went to the hospital to visit when one of our ladies became ill, and we surrounded each other with care when one of us went through the loss of a loved one. Most importantly, we each grew deeper in our faith and our love for Christ as we explored His Word together. Several women came to know what it meant to put their faith in Christ as a result of this one Bible study.

When we moved to another neighborhood, I jumped in and got involved with the homeowners' association again. I planned all the children's events, which allowed me to get to know the other mommies in the neighborhood. My involvement made it easy to invite the moms to a

Bible study at my home. We started the study over 25 years ago and now our kids are grown, but I still see the fruitfulness of the study in the lives of the ladies. Before coming to the group, several of the women didn't know that the Bible had anything to say to them personally, yet this small group study opened their eyes to God's love and a relationship with Him. I believe God places us in certain neighborhoods, so we will shine His light, but if we are busy running to our own activities, we miss the opportunity to reach into the lives of those who live closest to us.

May I encourage you to be prayerful about how God wants to use you in the place you are in right now. Whether it is your co-workers, or neighbors, ask the Lord to show you what He wants you to do to shine His light around you. It was a big step for me to pull out of the mega Bible study I was attending in order to start a neighborhood connection, but I'm so glad I did! Let's not become fat Christians, constantly consuming the great truths of the Bible but never using the principles of love to affect the lives around us. Ask the Lord where He wants you to start and reach out. If you need some help and encouragement, you can go to www .PositiveWomanConnection.me, a website I created to help encourage outreach Bible studies.

Reaching Out in Compassion

One of the most significant traits of believers is that of helping a brother or sister in need. Perhaps God is leading you to reach further than your neighborhood and into the lives of those with physical or financial needs. In their enlightening book *When Helping Hurts,* authors Steve Corbett and Brian Fikkert remind readers that the path to truly helping the materially poor is not through simply providing resources, but instead by walking with them in humble relationships. They define "poverty alleviation" as "the ministry of reconciliation: moving people closer to glorifying God by living in right relationship with God, with self, with others, and with the rest of creation."[2] They go on to say,

> The goal is not to make the materially poor all over the world into middle-to-upper-class North Americans, a group characterized by high rates of divorce, sexual addiction, substance abuse and mental illness. Nor is the

goal to make sure that the materially poor have enough money…Rather, the goal is to restore people to a full expression of humanness, to being what God created us all to be, people who glorify God by being in right relationship with God, with self, with others, and with the rest of creation.

When we approach compassion and service with a heart of humility, we are able to truly begin taking steps to lead those who are broken to the Savior. Sure we can help and assist with outward things, like food, clothing, parenting advice, and medical attention, but unless the inside is healed, unless Christ gives them a new direction, they will most likely fall back into their same old patterns. How do we truly help someone in need? We help by building a true, sincere, and lasting relationship with them. We help by assessing their physical needs and wisely teaching them and assisting them to be able to eventually help themselves. But most importantly, we help by pointing them to Christ.

One of the parables Jesus told was about being prepared for the final judgment. It is typically called the "Parable of the Sheep and the Goats," but I think I would title it "What Are You Doing in Jesus' Name?" Here are Jesus' words found in Matthew 25:31-46:

> When the Son of Man comes in his glory, and all the angels with him, he will sit on his glorious throne. All the nations will be gathered before him, and he will separate the people one from another as a shepherd separates the sheep from the goats. He will put the sheep on his right and the goats on his left.

> Then the King will say to those on his right, "Come, you who are blessed by my Father; take your inheritance, the kingdom prepared for you since the creation of the world. For I was hungry and you gave me something to eat, I was thirsty and you gave me something to drink, I was a stranger and you invited me in, I needed clothes and you clothed me, I was sick and you looked after me, I was in prison and you came to visit me."

Then the righteous will answer him, "Lord, when did we see you hungry and feed you, or thirsty and give you something to drink? When did we see you a stranger and invite you in, or needing clothes and clothe you? When did we see you sick or in prison and go to visit you?"

The King will reply, "Truly I tell you, whatever you did for one of the least of these brothers and sisters of mine, you did for me."

Then he will say to those on his left, "Depart from me, you who are cursed, into the eternal fire prepared for the devil and his angels. For I was hungry and you gave me nothing to eat, I was thirsty and you gave me nothing to drink, I was a stranger and you did not invite me in, I needed clothes and you did not clothe me, I was sick and in prison and you did not look after me."

They also will answer, "Lord, when did we see you hungry or thirsty or a stranger or needing clothes or sick or in prison, and did not help you?"

He will reply, "Truly I tell you, whatever you did not do for one of the least of these, you did not do for me."

Then they will go away to eternal punishment, but the righteous to eternal life.

Jesus wasn't just telling a sweet bedtime story here, He was sharing an action story. In this action story we are either in the one group or the other. Jesus is very serious about the love and compassion we show in His name, because it demonstrates the love and compassion He had toward us. We can't meet every need we see, but we can do something. We may not be able to reach thousands, but we can reach one person. It may mean that we must step out of our comfort zone. It may mean that we must be less busy and more aware of the needs around us. It may mean that we must stop and ask, "Lord, show me a life to touch and help. Love through me and make a difference."

True compassion means the desire to suffer with another person. The root word, *passion* actually means to suffer. Showing compassion isn't easy.

It's not something we do simply by writing a check and sending it in the mail. It could possibly mean that we get our hands dirty or that we build relationships with women on the other side of town. Compassion often means that we touch a life very different than our own. How has God gifted you? How can you use your gifts and talents to bring a cup of cold water to someone who is thirsty?

It begins with prayer, asking God to open our eyes to the needs around us. He will gladly guide us in how we can use our gifts and talents for kingdom purposes. Consider what would happen if every believer decided to reach out and touch one person in their city—one person who needs a good word, a smile, and some help? Let's do it! Let love and compassion begin with you and me reaching out to the one God has put in front of us and sincerely engage with the culture.

Digging Deeper

Read 1 John 3:16-18 and Acts 6:1-7. Pray and ask God to show you one way you can use the gifts and talents He has given you to touch and bless the lives of others. Write down what He shows you in your journal.

DISCUSS

1. What are some of the reasons Christians tend to not engage with the culture?

2. What is God showing you about how you can reach out in true compassion and touch the lives of those in need?

3. How does being a good listener open up doors to engage with the culture?

HELPFUL RESOURCES

- *When Helping Hurts* by Steve Corbett and Brian Fikkert
- *Toxic Charity* by Robert D. Lupton
- www.PositiveWomanConnection.me

13

Pray-pared for Each Day

This is the confidence we have in approaching God:
that if we ask anything according to his will, he hears us.
And if we know that he hears us—whatever we ask—we know that
we have what we asked of him.

1 JOHN 5:14-15

The mightier any is in the Word,
the more mighty he will be in prayer.

WILLIAM GURNALL

Amy is a wife and mother and actively involved in her neighborhood and Christian community. Several years ago she faced what she called "one of the darkest times of her life." She and her husband had to make some difficult decisions concerning one of their children, yet it was during this time that Amy experienced an extraordinary sense of God's presence, strength, and comfort. I'll let her tell you her story.

> My husband and I had to make some of the hardest decisions in our parenting history, and we were already feeling pretty depleted. We received a call that demanded our immediate attention, and we knew we needed to jump into action. Yet on this particular occasion, my husband took the front line, and I stayed at home. I wanted to be on the front lines though. I wanted to be able to help and fix the situation. I was conflicted.
>
> Then God shifted my focus to what I *could* do. I pulled out my Bible and went and prayed. I poured out my heart to God for our child. I had no idea what I should read for "such a time as this" and so I resorted to the "close your

eyes, let your Bible fall open, and see where it takes you" technique.

The pages fell open to 2 Chronicles 20. A place I didn't remember ever going to before. It was the most amazing chapter and was speaking to *exactly* what I needed. Words popped off the page at me like

"*Alarmed*, Jehoshaphat *resolved* to *inquire* of the Lord"

"'*We have no power* to face this vast army that is attacking us'"

"'We don't know what to do but *our eyes are on you*'"

"'*Do not be afraid* or *discouraged* because of this vast army'"

"'For *the battle is not yours but God's*'"

"Jehoshaphat *bowed* with his face to the ground"

"'Have faith in the Lord your God and *you will be upheld*'"

"'*Praise him* for the splendor of his holiness'"

"'*Give thanks* to the Lord, for his love endures forever'"

"*As they began* to sing and *praise*, the Lord set ambushes and [the enemy] was defeated"

I was overwhelmed with emotion, with gratitude and awe. My God had taken me right where I needed to be: to be reminded of just what I needed to be reminded of, to be encouraged and to feel loved and cared for. I didn't feel left out because I wasn't on the front lines anymore. I felt empowered to pray with all I had and stay connected to God and whatever He was trying to show me for our family. I felt the peace of God because I paused long enough to read His Word and let Him speak to me through it. Now, I encourage others with these somewhat obscure verses when they are in "times of trouble."

The Battle Is the Lord's

Amy's story is a powerful reminder to us that the greatest work we can do is on our knees. Let's take a moment to examine the story Amy read in 2 Chronicles 20:1-26 and see what it can mean in our own personal prayer time. The narrative opens with an extremely difficult situation for God's people. The Israelites were surrounded by a vast army that had come against King Jehoshaphat. The Bible tells us that the king resolved to inquire of the Lord and declared a fast for all of Judah. People gathered from every town in Judah to seek help from the Lord. Jehoshaphat offered a prayer for the people at the temple. Here's how he started out:

> "LORD, the God of our ancestors, are you not the God who
> is in heaven? You rule over all the kingdoms of the nations.
> Power and might are in your hand, and no one can with-
> stand you. Our God, did you not drive out the inhabitants
> of this land before your people Israel and give it forever to
> the descendants of Abraham your friend? They have lived
> in it and have built in it a sanctuary for your Name, saying,
> 'If calamity comes upon us, whether the sword of judgment,
> or plague or famine, we will stand in your presence before
> this temple that bears your Name and will cry out to you
> in our distress, and you will hear us and save us.'"

He praised God and reflected on the mighty things He had done in the past. Jehoshaphat went on with his request, "For we have no power to face this vast army that is attacking us. We do not know what to do, but our eyes are on you." Did you notice King Jehoshaphat's humility before God? His words, "We do not know what to do, but our eyes are on you," certainly reveal his dependence on God. Often we tend to avoid prayer because we think we know what to do. We even think we know exactly how God should fix it. Here we see the complete humility and dependence of the king on God. He is leaning His full weight into God Almighty. Peter wrote about humility in prayer saying this, "Humble yourselves, therefore, under the mighty hand of God so that at the proper time he may exalt you, casting all your anxieties on him, because he cares for you" (1 Peter 5:6-7). The greatest act of humility is casting our cares on Him instead of pridefully assuming we know it all.

We also see the importance of community as Jehoshaphat brought the people together to pray. Our personal prayer life is vital, and yet corporate prayer is also important as we join together to humbly seek God and rejoice in His work. As they were gathered, the Spirit of the Lord came on a man named Jahaziel. Here's what God said through him:

> "Listen, King Jehoshaphat and all who live in Judah and Jerusalem! This is what the LORD says to you: 'Do not be afraid or discouraged because of this vast army. For the battle is not yours, but God's. Tomorrow march down against them. They will be climbing up by the Pass of Ziz, and you will find them at the end of the gorge in the Desert of Jeruel. You will not have to fight this battle. Take up your positions; stand firm and see the deliverance the LORD will give you, Judah and Jerusalem. Do not be afraid; do not be discouraged. Go out to face them tomorrow, and the LORD will be with you.'"

Like my friend Amy, I think we need that same kind of reminder. We want to fight our own battles so we can fix things ourselves. But when we humbly give our battles over to the Lord in prayer, He gives us direction and He also fights for us. Jehoshaphat bowed down and worshipped the Lord along with all the people of Judah. Here's what King Jehoshaphat did the next morning.

> Early in the morning they left for the Desert of Tekoa. As they set out, Jehoshaphat stood and said, "Listen to me, Judah and people of Jerusalem! Have faith in the LORD your God and you will be upheld; have faith in his prophets and you will be successful." After consulting the people, Jehoshaphat appointed men to sing to the LORD and to praise him for the splendor of his holiness as they went out at the head of the army, saying:
>
> > "Give thanks to the LORD,
> >   for his love endures forever."

Jehoshaphat encouraged the people to sing praises and have faith, before the prayer was answered! There's another powerful lesson—don't wait for the happy answer before you start praising God. God deserves our praise whether He answers exactly the way we asked or not. Praise and thanksgiving are essential elements in our prayer life. If we want to be strong prayer warriors, we must be faithful praise givers. The Bible tells us that as they began to sing and praise the Lord, God set ambushes against Judah's enemies and they defeated them. The narrative ends as the armies of Judah gathered the plunder. It took three days to collect it all, and on the fourth day they assembled once again and praised the Lord together.

God did more than they asked or imagined. Not only did He protect them, He blessed them with plunder. I am reminded of Paul's prayer found in Ephesians, "Now to him who is able to do immeasurably more than all we ask or imagine, according to his power that is at work within us, to him be glory in the church and in Christ Jesus throughout all generations, for ever and ever! Amen" (Ephesians 3:20-21). Our greatest battleground is on our knees, God is fighting for us in ways beyond what we can ask or imagine. Do not be afraid, my friend, if the battle you are facing seems overwhelming. Remember this great truth from God's Word: "Do not be afraid or discouraged because of this vast army. For the battle is not yours, but God's." May we carry that message in our hearts continually as we give every aspect of our day over to Him.

Will God Answer My Prayers?

Think of the powerful principles on prayer that we learned from just one Old Testament story! Do you want to know how to pray more effectively? Silly question, right? Who doesn't want to see their prayers answered? A *Newsweek* poll titled "Is God Listening?" showed that of those who do pray, 87 percent believed that God answers their prayers at least some of the time. Our question may not be, "Does God answer prayer?" Deep down inside our ultimate question is, "Will He answer *my* prayers?" We have all had times when we prayed for something and didn't seem to get the answer that we were hoping for, making us question, "Did I pray the right way? Is God mad at me? Did He really hear me? Why does He answer some of my prayers and not others?"

The Bible is our guidebook for prayer. In it we not only see powerful examples of answered prayer, but we also find the teachings of Jesus on how to pray effectively. We discover God's invitation to prayer and His desire for us to cast our cares on Him. We also learn some of the reasons why prayers may not be answered exactly how we had wished.

In this chapter we are going to explore what the Bible has to teach us about the power and passion of prayer. My hope is that this chapter will encourage your heart and strengthen your prayer life. I find it humbling to think that Almighty God invites us to pray. He loves us and cares about the details of our lives. From Genesis to Revelation we find examples of God listening to His people and answering their prayers.

Our opening verse in this chapter reminds us, "If we ask anything according to his will, he hears us. And if we know that he hears us—whatever we ask—we know that we have what we asked of him." How do we know we are praying according to God's will? His will is revealed in His Word, so if we are going to pray according to His will, we must pray according to His Word. Certainly we don't find a listing of His will for every detail or every circumstance of our lives, yet the more we know of His Word, the more we come to understand His heart of love. We learn who He is and how He works, and we surrender our will to His. We want to approach God's throne with confidence, so let's look at what the Scriptures have to teach us about this glorious invitation of prayer.

The Bible is filled with treasured prayers, in fact there are over 200 prayers recorded in it. We learn how to pray effectively as we observe God's people praying. There are several women who offered powerful prayers of praise and thanksgiving in both the Old and New Testaments. Since praise is one of the most important elements of prayer, I encourage you to read their prayers and consider how you can write a similar prayer of praise for what God has done in your life.

- The song of Moses and Miriam (Exodus 15:1-18)
- The song of Deborah (Judges 5:1-31)
- Hannah's prayer (1 Samuel 2:1-10)
- The Magnificat: Mary's song of praise (Luke 1:46-55)

The Perfect Prayer Warrior

If you want to know how to do something, consult the experts. When it comes to prayer, Jesus not only knew everything there was to know about prayer, but He practiced it Himself. And by the way, doesn't that boggle your mind to think that the Son of God spent time in prayer? He knew that time with His Father was essential in order for Him to walk in obedience and carry out the plans the Father had for Him. The Bible tells us that Jesus got up while it was still dark and went to a solitary place where He prayed (Mark 1:35) Let's learn from the Master! One of Jesus' most in-depth discourses on prayer can be found in the Sermon on the Mount. Here, Jesus gives us instructions in prayer as well as a sample prayer (known as the Lord's Prayer).

> When you pray, do not be like the hypocrites, for they love to pray standing in the synagogues and on the street corners to be seen by others. Truly I tell you, they have received their reward in full. But when you pray, go into your room, close the door, and pray to your Father, who is unseen. Then your Father, who sees what is done in secret, will reward you. And when you pray, do not keep on babbling like pagans, for they think they will be heard because of their many words. Do not be like them, for your Father knows what you need before you ask him.
>
> This, then, is how you should pray:
>
> > Our Father in heaven,
> > hallowed be your name, your kingdom come,
> > your will be done,
> >   on earth as it is in heaven.
> > Give us today our daily bread.
> > And forgive us our debts,
> >   as we also have forgiven our debtors.
> > And lead us not into temptation,
> >   but deliver us from the evil one.
>
> For if you forgive other people when they sin against you, your heavenly Father will also forgive you. But if you do not forgive others their sins, your Father will not forgive your sins (Matthew 6:5-15).

This was an example of how we should pray. Jesus didn't intend for us to simply recite this prayer over and over again, but rather to use it as an example to understand how to pray; praising the Father, seeking His will, asking for provision, forgiveness, and direction. Notice the emphasis on forgiveness. Forgiveness is an important part of our obedience to God and our prayer life. Jesus also encouraged His followers to ask, seek, and knock:

> Ask and it will be given to you; seek and you will find; knock and the door will be opened to you. For everyone who asks receives; the one who seeks finds; and to the one who knocks, the door will be opened. Which of you, if your son asks for bread, will give him a stone? Or if he asks for a fish, will give him a snake? If you, then, though you are evil, know how to give good gifts to your children, how much more will your Father in heaven give good gifts to those who ask him! (Matthew 7:7-11).

Do you sense God's care for His children? What a beautiful and open invitation to bring our cares to the Father. Jesus taught about prayer through parables as well:

- In Luke 11:5-8 Jesus told the story of the friend asking for bread at midnight, teaching boldness in prayer.
- In Luke 18:1-8 Jesus taught persistence in prayer using the story of a widow who persistently sought justice from a judge.

Possibly the most beautiful and passionate of Jesus' prayers is found in John 17, as John records Jesus' prayer for Himself, for His disciples, and for future believers (us!). More than any other lesson, Jesus demonstrated His obedience to His Father through prayer when He was in the garden, approaching His final hour. *"Abba*, Father, everything is possible for you. Take this cup from me. Yet not what I will, but what you will" (Mark 14:35-36). May our prayers always have that same heartbeat—not our will but His. Acquiescing in our own desires to His, this is the true model of prayer. May His will be done. Prayer is not simply bringing our wants to God. Prayer is a joining of our hearts with His.

The Apostle Paul's Prayers

Why was the apostle Paul so effective in his ministry? I believe it was because he was an effective prayer warrior. He started most of his epistles by letting his fellow believers know that he prayed for them all the time. Often he would tell them exactly what he was praying. For instance, to the Ephesians he wrote,

> And this is my prayer: that your love may abound more and more in knowledge and depth of insight, so that you may be able to discern what is best and may be pure and blameless for the day of Christ, filled with the fruit of righteousness that comes through Jesus Christ—to the glory and praise of God (Philippians 1:9-11).

Now that's a powerful prayer to pray for someone else or even for yourself. I've found that this prayer, as well as many of Paul's other prayers throughout the New Testament, offers a great template to pray for my kids or husband or fellow believers. Here is a list of Paul's prayers in the Bible. I encourage you to look them up, mark them up, and pray them up!

- Romans 1:8-10; 10:1; 15:5-6, 13
- 2 Corinthians 9:12-15; 12:7-9; 13:7-9
- Galatians 6:18
- Ephesians 1:3; 1:15-23; 3:14-21
- Philippians 1:3-6; 1:9-11
- Colossians 1:3-14
- 1 Thessalonians 3:9-13; 5:23-24; 28
- 2 Thessalonians 1:11-12; 2:16-17; 3:16
- 1 Timothy 1:12; 2:1-2
- 2 Timothy 1:3-7
- Philemon 1:4-6

Also, you may want to pray through Paul's description of the armor of God found in Ephesians 6:10-18. We know we are praying in His will when we are praying His Word. If you want to pray with confidence, then pray the prayers you find in Scriptures. Pray His promises. As we become women of the Word through our own reading and studying, we also become women of prayer. We learn how to pray with power and humility as we praise Him and seek His will. Paul gave us this charge: "Rejoice always, pray continually, give thanks in all circumstances; for this is God's will for you in Christ Jesus" (1 Thessalonians 5:16-18).

Spurgeon wrote,

> Prayer must not be our chance work, but our daily business, our habit and vocation. As artists give themselves to their models, and poets to their classical pursuits, so must we addict ourselves to prayer. We must be immersed in prayer as in our element, and so pray without ceasing. Lord, teach us so to pray that we may be more and more prevalent in supplication.[1]

Digging Deeper

Read John 17, known as Jesus' high priestly prayer. Record in your journal all that you learn about prayer and about Jesus' love for His followers.

DISCUSS

1. How do the prayers in the Bible encourage your prayer life?

2. What is the most important aspect of prayer to you?

3. What are some of the distractions that may tend to keep you from prayer and how can you resolve them?

HELPFUL RESOURCES

- *Power of Persistent Prayer* by Cindy Jacobs
- *Praying God's Word for Your Life* by Kathi Lipp
- *Praying the Bible into Your Life* by Stormie Omartian

Woman of the Word

Natalie is a godly young lady who works in the trauma ICU as a registered nurse in Dallas. Several years ago she was diagnosed with ulcerative colitis, a digestive autoimmune disease. I've asked her if I could share one of her blog posts specifically concerning answered prayer and healing.

Everyone copes with disease and trial differently. For me, I rely on my faith in Jesus Christ. Even if you don't agree with it, take it as my way of explaining how I cope with the trials of chronic illness (and everyday life). My relationship with the Lord has given me more joy and hope than I could ever imagine.

Every January our church focuses on a month of prayer. Not like we don't advocate prayer at all times of the year, but it's a specified time to home in on prayer as a great advantage and powerful resource. As I sat in church listening to the pastor speak on the importance and effectiveness of asking the Lord, I felt very convicted. How much time do I spend altering our diet, cooking, reading about medications, and so son? And, in comparison, how much time do I spend asking the Lord for one simple thing: healing?

I believe in the power of prayer. I've seen dramatic changes occur in my life when I pray in faith. So why do I not expend the same amount of time and effort on a task ultimately more powerful than any food or medication? Because I fall into the human trap of monotony. At the beginning of any trial, you adamantly throw yourself into the suffering, completely consumed by whatever mountain of hardship you face. You pray earnestly on your knees, desperate for a solution. But over time, especially as things improve or grow consistent, we forget to continue to bother the Lord with our requests. We think, "Well, if He hasn't done it by now, He won't do it" or "What's the point anymore if I haven't seen the results I wanted?"

First of all, this logic is not only foolish, but also selfish, and I have to admonish myself regularly not to indulge in it. Just because the Lord hasn't completely healed me at this point doesn't mean that He's not granting me a measure of healing (which I've clearly seen over the past year). He's already given humanity medications and knowledge for healing that He didn't have to give. And His timing is not our timing. We want instant results; He sees all things and intends to give blessings at the proper time. His omniscience supersedes our lowly human understanding. If we always got what we desired right away, we would turn into a very selfish people, seeking the Lord only for His gifts, rather than Himself. I'm pretty positive I would view the Lord that way in my sinful humanity. The point is, maybe one day the Lord will grant me full and total healing, maybe He won't. Either way I should pray.[2]

You can read Natalie's blog at www.ThirtyEightFive.com ("Thirty-EightFive" stands for Isaiah 38:5).

14

The Heart of Worship

Ascribe to the LORD the glory due his name;
worship the LORD in the splendor of his holiness.

PSALM 29:2

Where God is truly known,
He is necessarily adored.

A.W. PINK

*M*iley, a female husky, was living—or perhaps I should say barely surviving—in a trash dump somewhere near Los Angeles. A rescuer from Hope for Paws learned about her and went to check out the situation. It was worse than he thought. Miley could barely lift her head and was in terrible need of medical attention, suffering from mange, malnutrition, parasites, and infections. The rescuer realized that Miley would die a painful death if she stayed in this situation, so his first step was to gain the dog's trust and confidence. Despite deplorable conditions and filth, the merciful rescuer sat down with Miley for several hours there in the dump. Eventually he gained Miley's trust and was able to coax her into his car and get her to the vet.

The first few days were spent giving Miley medical attention and letting her rest so her body could heal. By the third day, Miley had enough energy to offer precious kisses to her kind rescuer.[1] She continued on her road to recovery, getting better, day by day. Perhaps you are wondering what in the world a story about a dog is doing in a chapter about worship? Well, it's a rather interesting correlation. You see, the Greek word for *worship* is *proskuneo,* which means "to kiss." It is most likely derived from the word *kuon,* meaning "dog." Strong's Greek dictionary says *proskuneo* reflects the image of a dog licking its master's hand. How precious to picture Miley gratefully licking the hand of her rescuer! Yet our story of salvation is not too different than Miley's. The Bible reminds us that we have been rescued from the dominion of darkness and brought into the kingdom of light. Like Miley, we too needed rescuing.

We couldn't save ourselves, but God in His kindness came to this earth in the form of a man. I picture Miley's rescuer sitting there in the dump with her, and I think about Jesus who left His heavenly throne to come to this earth and live among us. Miley was destined to die in the trash heap, but thankfully she placed her trust in the rescuer. The Bible says that once we were dead in our sins, but now we have been made alive in Christ. He rescued us and cleansed us through His blood shed on the cross. Our response through worship should be as sweet and endearing as a dog licking its rescuer's hand in gratitude and honor.

What a unique and interesting way to understand worship. Often we associate worship with singing music at church, but worship is so much more than simply singing songs. Worship is an attitude of the heart and singing is an outward expression of the adoration within us. At the very heart of worship are a deep respect, reverence, and gratitude for who God is and what He has done for us. British pastor Geoffrey B. Wilson said, "Worship is the only fitting response to God's bounty."[2] Worship honors God's glory and rejoices in His kindness toward us.

There are many examples of worship throughout God's Word, but one that I often think about is in Isaiah. Here's what the prophet wrote about a vision he had:

> I saw the LORD, high and exalted, seated on a throne; and the train of his robe filled the temple. Above him were seraphim, each with six wings: With two wings they covered their faces, with two they covered their feet, and with two they were flying. And they were calling to one another:
>
> "Holy, holy, holy is the LORD Almighty;
> the whole earth is full of his glory."
>
> At the sound of their voices the doorposts and thresholds shook and the temple was filled with smoke.

"Woe to me!" I cried. "I am ruined! For I am a man of unclean lips, and I live among a people of unclean lips, and my eyes have seen the King, the LORD Almighty."

Then one of the seraphim flew to me with a live coal in his hand, which he had taken with tongs from the altar. With it he touched my mouth and said, "See, this has touched your lips; your guilt is taken away and your sin atoned for" (Isaiah 6:1-7).

Isaiah must have been overwhelmed at God's glory and humbled by his own humanity. When we turn our eyes toward God and consider His holiness, righteousness, majesty, and splendor, we can't help but overflow with praise for who He is and yet also grieve over the sins we have committed. The angels declared, "Holy, Holy, Holy!" the threefold repetition intensifies the power of the word itself. In Hebrew literature a word was repeated to show emphasis. Holiness refers to absolute purity. The word itself means "separate or one set apart." The repetition "Holy, Holy, Holy," can only be spoken of God Himself.

The natural response to recognizing His holiness is to also acknowledge our sinfulness. Worship involves praise and adoration, as well as humility and thanksgiving. When I praise God, I can't help but come to a point of confession about my own sin against Him as Isaiah did. Confession is a natural part of our worship before God because we are agreeing with God about our sin. The angel brought a hot stone to atone for Isaiah's sin, and yet as believers in Christ our sins have been atoned for once and for all. Confession simply means we are agreeing with God that we have sinned. Confession leads us to a place of overwhelming gratitude for all Christ did for us on the cross.

Praise, confession, and thanksgiving are all three bound together in worship. Worship isn't about the perfect songs or ceremonies, it's about a heart that desires to honor and glorify a holy God. In Isaiah's vision he heard the voice of the Lord saying, "Whom shall I send and who will go for us?" Isaiah's immediate and worshipful response was, "Here I am! Send me." Worship brings us to a point of laying down our lives in service and obedience to our great and mighty King. A true heart of worship leads us away from being self-serving and leads us toward being God-serving.

Paul wrote in his letter to the Romans, "I urge you, brothers and sisters, in view of God's mercy, to offer your bodies as a living sacrifice, holy and pleasing to God—this is your true and proper worship" (Romans 12:1). Worship is a laying down of our hearts in obedience to God. It is an attitude of surrender.

God Loves This

Imagine going to a party honoring one of your friends. And yet while you were there at the party, all you did was complain that the cake wasn't *your* favorite cake and the presents were not what *you* wanted. How crazy would that be? The party wasn't about *you*; it was about your friend who was being honored. Often we miss the point of worship on Sunday. It's not about the type of music we prefer or the pastor's perfectly entertaining message, it's about coming to God with a heart of adoration and praise as well as confession and thanksgiving. The music is an outward demonstration of what should be going on in our hearts continually. The sermon is an opportunity to listen to the Word of God and learn more about the heart and the will of God. It's His party, and it ought to be all about Him.

God does not take worship lightly. In Matthew 15 we read about the Pharisees approaching Jesus and asking why His disciples break the tradition of the elders by not washing their hands when they eat. They were more concerned about the outward appearances than their inward attitudes toward God. Jesus rebuked them, quoting Isaiah:

> "These people honor me with their lips,
>   but their hearts are far from me.
> They worship me in vain;
>   their teachings are merely human rules"
> (Matthew 15:8-9).

So what is it that God desires from us when it comes to worship? Jesus talked about God's desire for worship during His conversation with the woman at the well. As a despised Samaritan woman, her people worshipped on a mountain, but the Jews worshipped in Jerusalem. This was one of the points of contention between the Jews and the Samaritans.

Jesus taught her that the location of worship is not nearly as important as the heart of the worshipper. Here's what Jesus said to her:

> Woman, believe me, the hour is coming when neither on this mountain nor in Jerusalem will you worship the Father. You worship what you do not know; we worship what we know, for salvation is from the Jews. But the hour is coming, and is now here, when the true worshipers will worship the Father in spirit and truth, for the Father is seeking such people to worship him. God is spirit, and those who worship him must worship in spirit and truth (John 4:21-24 ESV).

As a spiritual being, God is not limited to one place. He can be worshipped at any place at any time. So I must ask myself, "Do I live with a genuine heart of worship—a heart that loves and adores Him—or am I simply pretending on Sunday mornings that He is my Lord and Master?" To worship God in both spirit and in truth means that I worship Him with both my mind (what I know as true from God's Word) and I worship Him from my heart in the power of His Spirit. The word for *spirit* used in the New Testament is *pneuma* and is used in some places in the New Testament to refer to our disposition and attitude, but it is used in other places to refer to God's Spirit.

God's Spirit helps us to worship by interceding for us (Romans 8:26), by teaching us about Christ (John 14:26), by reminding us that we are loved (Romans 5:5), and by testifying with our spirit that we are God's children (Romans 8:16). The word *enthusiasm* comes to mind. Enthusiasm means "God in us," so when I think of worshipping in spirit, I think of worshipping with enthusiasm. Worship should be a joyful experience overflowing from a heart filled with gratitude and praise. Remember the dog metaphor? Think about the enthusiasm with which a dog greets its master. How wonderful to have that same heart of enthusiasm when we greet our Lord.

Worshipping in both spirit and in truth is an important balance. The Bible tells us to love God with all our heart, soul, mind, and strength. When we worship with our whole heart, we worship with enthusiasm, but not at the expense of our minds. Feelings can take us down many diverse paths if we are not allowing them to be grounded in the truth—God's truth. Yet the Pharisees were so caught up in the laws, rituals, and mental assent of worship that they missed the heart of worship—Jesus Himself. So let us worship in both spirit and in truth, with our hearts and with our heads.

A Picture of Worship

In Nehemiah we find an interesting worship service, which involves both enthusiasm and the reading of God's Word. The service began when Ezra, the scribe, stood on a platform to read the book of the Law to God's people. As he opened the book, all the people stood up in reverence. Ezra praised the Lord and all the people lifted their hands and responded, "Amen! Amen!" Then they bowed down and worshipped the Lord with their faces to the ground. The word for *worshipped* here is the Hebrew word *shachah*, which means "to prostrate or bow down in homage." God's people were bowing in a show of obeisance to God, recognizing His holiness.

Next, the Levites instructed the people in the Law while the people stood and listened. They read from the book of the Law of God (the Pentateuch, the first five books of the Bible), making it clear and giving the meaning so that the people could understand what was being read. Such a beautiful reminder that God wants us to know and understand His Word! Do you want to know how the people responded to hearing it? They began weeping. Yes, weeping and mourning in recognition of God's holiness and how far they had gone astray from His laws. It reminds me of Isaiah's reaction that we read earlier in the chapter. Yet God does not intend for us to remain in our sorrow over our sin. He is a redeeming God and brings atonement for His people.

Finally, Nehemiah, Ezra, and the Levites all said in unison, "This day is sacred to the LORD your God. Do not mourn or weep." Nehemiah went on to say, "Go and enjoy choice food and sweet drinks, and send some to those who have nothing prepared. This day is holy to our LORD. Do not grieve, for the joy of the LORD is your strength." The people went on to celebrate with great joy. It was the joy of the Lord that gave them strength. Isn't that a beautiful picture of worship, especially as God's redeemed people? There is great joy, enthusiasm, and thanksgiving when we recognize God has redeemed us through the blood of Christ. When we understand God's holiness and our sinfulness, we can't help but celebrate with enthusiasm. The joy of the Lord is our strength!

Prison Praise

One of the best worship services in the Bible occurred in the worst of circumstances. In Acts 16 we read that Paul and Silas were severely beaten and thrown in prison. Not only were they beaten and thrown in prison for doing something noble, but they were also placed in the inner part of the prison and their feet were placed in stocks. Now what would you do in a situation like this? Grumble and complain? I'm pretty sure I would! Yet, Paul and Silas chose to worship God there in the deepest, darkest prison, with feet in stocks. Worship is a great antidote for grumbling.

The Bible tells us that the prisoners listened intently to Paul and Silas. As the two prayed and sang hymns of praise to God, a great earthquake shook the very foundations of the prison and all the doors were opened and everyone's bonds were unfastened. None of the prisoners ran away—perhaps because they saw the power of God in the lives of two crazy worshippers. Even the prison guard came to know Christ. Instead of wasting their time in prison simply fretting and fearing, Paul and Silas started praying and praising. What a great example for us as well!

In my own life, I have seen God calm my fears and set my heart at rest when I praise and worship Him in the midst of my challenges. My friend, I want to encourage you, when you are riddled by the destructive thoughts of fear or despair, turn your eyes upward and begin praising God for who He is and what He is able to do. Fears so easily pop into our thought-lives, and if we are not careful they can begin to dominate our minds. At that moment, allow your heart to worship Him. Praise Him that He knows all things, He can see all things, and He can do whatever He wants. Give Him glory for His sovereignty, majesty, love, and compassion. What a privilege that He invites us, His people, to approach His throne and worship Him.

May our lives be a song of worship as we live for His glory! We don't have to wait until church on Sunday to worship God. As Paul said, "Always give thanks to God the Father for everything." We can worship God day and night. Although it may seem counterintuitive, we can praise God even in our challenges and difficulties as we turn our hearts toward Him and recognize His ability to do all things. The opposite of worship would be to live with an attitude of pride, arrogance, fear, and self-centeredness. A woman who lives with an attitude of worship is a beautiful woman indeed. Proverbs tells us, "Charm is deceitful and beauty is vain, but a woman who fears God, she shall be praised."

Digging Deeper

Read Psalms 12, 96, 98, 99, 100. Record everything you learn about worship and about God's attributes from these Psalms.

DISCUSS

1. How would you describe true worship in your own life?

2. What are some typical reasons that we do not maintain an attitude of worship?

3. Why is humility an important aspect of worship?

HELPFUL RESOURCES

- *The Purpose of Man: Designed to Worship* by A.W. Tozer
- *Engaging with God, A Biblical Theology of Worship* by David Peterson
- *Christ-Centered Worship* by Bryan Chapell

15

Church Redefined

He [Christ] is before all things, and in him all things hold together.
And he is the head of the body, the church.

COLOSSIANS 1:17-18

The church was originated not only by Christ,
but also from him, and cannot continue to exist
for even a moment apart from him.

R.B. KUIPER

Possibly one of the most misunderstood words in the English language is the word *church*. For much of my life I thought church was a building with a steeple where I attended services on Sunday mornings in order to worship God. Remember the little poem with hand motions that we used to say as children? "This is the church, this is the steeple, open the door and see all the people." When you hear the word *church*, what comes to your mind? To some people, church has a negative connotation, conjuring up bad memories or past hurts. I hope this chapter will help you see church in a new light and from a fresh and positive perspective. Let's examine what the Bible says about the church.

The word *church* is used 80 times in the New Testament and is derived from the Greek word *ekklesia*, which means "an assembly" or "called-out ones." It stresses a group of people called out for a special purpose. Strong's says the church (*ekklesia*) represented "the new society of which Jesus was the founder, being as it was a society knit together by the closest spiritual bonds and altogether independent of space."[1] So what is the membership requirement to be a part of this society called the church? It is to believe on the name of the Lord Jesus Christ, trusting Him as your Lord and Savior. We join with no merit of our own; it is because of Christ that we are members. I like how pastor Charles Clayton Morrison put it: "The

Christian church is the only society in the world in which membership is based upon the qualification that the candidate shall be unworthy of membership."[2]

Erik Thoennes of Talbot Theological Seminary writes, "The church is the community of God's redeemed people—all who have truly trusted Christ alone for their salvation. It is created by the Holy Spirit to exalt Jesus Christ as Lord of all."[3] In reality, there is only one church, the global community of believers on earth and in heaven, and yet we have an abundance of local church bodies. Calvin distinguished between the local church and the global church using the terms "visible church" meaning the church we can see on earth, and the "invisible church" meaning true believers (the elect) who are part of the body of Christ. Only God, who knows our hearts, knows the ultimate makeup of the invisible church. As Paul wrote, "The Lord knows those who are his" (2 Timothy 2:19).

Within the "visible church" (the local churches), we may find believers along with those who only look like believers. Many people play church. They look good on the outside, going to church services and even doing myriad good things, but they do not know Christ or submit to His Lordship. In His Sermon on the Mount, Jesus warned about false prophets that come to us in sheep's clothing but inwardly are ravenous wolves (Matthew 7:15-17). He also warned of those who do mighty works in His name, yet He will declare to them, "I never knew you" (Matthew 7:21-23). When we place our faith in Christ as our Redeemer and Lord, we become a part of His family (John 1:12). We come to know God, not by our works of righteousness, but by faith in His righteousness (Philippians 3:9-10).

Common Connection

Faith in Christ connects us with all believers under the Lordship of Christ. The Bible tells us that the church is the body of Christ and that He is the head of the body (Ephesians 1:22-23; Colossians 1:18). As the body of Christ we are under Christ's authority, and we work together using the gifts God has given us. Second Corinthians reminds us that God has given us gifts not to use for our own personal edification, but rather to build up the body of Christ—to build up His church. God often gives us physical pictures to help us understand spiritual truths, and He chose to use the body as a metaphor of the church body. Just as in a healthy body, all of its members work in harmony for the good of the body, so under the authority of Christ, we should work together using our gifts to strengthen the church as a whole.

The Bible also uses the metaphor of a bride to describe the church (2 Corinthians 11:2; Ephesians 5:32; Revelation 19:7; 21:9). I love the picture of Christ as the groom and believers as His bride, because it demonstrates a faithful covenant love relationship between Christ and His church. The relationship between Christ and His church is a beautiful and everlasting one. Do you sense that the foundational trait of the church is love—loving God with all our heart and loving our brothers and sisters in Christ with a selfless love as well? Love should be the hallmark of the church. The world should know us by our love—our love for Christ, our love for our brothers and sisters in Christ and our love for those who don't know Christ.

Often we talk about going *to* church and sitting *in* church, but perhaps we should talk about *being* the church. What exactly does it look like to *be* the church? Canon Ernest Southcott (founder of the "home church" movement in England) said, "The holiest moment of the church service is the moment when God's people—strengthened by preaching and sacrament—go out of the church door into the world to be the church. We don't go to church; we are the church."[4] As we are strengthened by the work of our local churches (the visible church), let us go out into the world and live out the love we have received. Our job as Christ's body, the church, is to show the world what Jesus' love looks like in word and in deed.

John said it plain and clear, "Dear friends, since God so loved us, we also ought to love one another. No one has ever seen God; but if we love one another, God lives in us and his love is made complete in us" (1 John 4:7-12). When we demonstrate Christ's love, we are truly *being* the church. We are His hands, His feet, His heart, His mouth. Francis Schaeffer put it this way: "We cannot expect the world to believe that the Father sent the Son, that Jesus' claims are true and that Christianity is true, unless the world sees some reality of the oneness of true Christians."[5] The world will be drawn to Christ, not by our perfect words or our incredible church services. They will see Christ through the love we have for one another.

Why Go to Church?

If the church is defined by the believers in Christ, is it really necessary to join together in a church building once a week? And what about the early church, who met in houses, not steepled buildings? What's the point of coming together? The author of Hebrews wrote:

> Let us hold unswervingly to the hope we profess, for he who promised is faithful. And let us consider how we may spur one another on toward love and good deeds, not giving up meeting together, as some are in the habit of doing, but encouraging one another—and all the more as you see the Day approaching (Hebrews 10:23-25).

The church was not meant to live in isolation, but rather to join together to encourage one another. As iron sharpens iron, so one person sharpens another. We need connection, encouragement, and fellowship with our family, our brothers and sisters in Christ. The connection we experience with other believers is a spiritual connection, a bond based on our common love for Christ. We live in this world, but we are citizens of another world. Paul wrote, "Our citizenship is in heaven," and as citizens of another land, we must come together to build each other up.

Not only do we join together for encouragement, but we join together for growth. The purpose of a church service is not to fill seats and entertain enormous numbers of people. Rather it ought to be a time for the perfecting (or equipping) of the saints (Ephesians 4:12). *Perfecting* means helping God's people grow in righteousness as they hear a message of conviction from God's Word. We don't want to waste time developing shallow Christians who have a weak view of God. We want to encourage true growth, rooted and founded on knowing the Bible and experiencing salvation in Christ. Coming together as a church was never meant to be a time to encourage wimpy Christianity, rather it was meant to be a time to challenge and strengthen believers in their faith.

I think about John Calvin, who dedicated his life to making the mind of God understandable to the mind of man. Brandon Crawford writes,

> For Calvin, true wisdom can be attained only through the knowledge of the One true God. And only when that

God is seen in the fullness of His majesty can man really understand who he is and what he is to do. Further, Calvin believed that the only source for attaining the knowledge of God was the Bible, God's revelation of Himself to mankind.[6]

Which leads me to the most important reason we come together as a body of believers—and that is to glorify God. As we study His Word, we begin to recognize the glory and majesty of God. Our response is to worship Him. The psalmist wrote,

> Come, let us bow down in worship,
>   let us kneel before the LORD our Maker;
> for he is our God
>   and we are the people of his pasture,
>   the flock under his care
> (Psalm 95:6-7).

As His beloved flock, let us come together to glorify our Great Shepherd and to feed in the delicious meadow of His Word. How beautiful is Christ's church, glorifying God and growing in the Word! I hope this chapter and this entire book inspires you to be the church as you participate in studying the Scriptures and falling in love with the Lord more deeply every day. Please keep in touch and let me know how your journey of growth in the Bible is going. You can follow me in a variety of ways on my website: www.PositiveLifePrinciples.com. I look forward to staying connected!

Digging Deeper

Read Ephesians 4 and write in your journal all that you learn about being the body of Christ, the church.

DISCUSS

1. In what way are you connected to the visible church in your city?

2. How are you using your spiritual gifts to build up the body?

3. Knowing that we are the body of Christ, how should you work and interact with our Christian brothers and sisters?

HELPFUL RESOURCES

- *What Is the Church?* by R.C. Sproul
- *The True Church* by J. C. Ryle
- *The Body* by Charles Colson

Good to Know

Bonus Help and Information

⟨∼⟩

*E*veryone loves to get a little more than they paid for, right? Although I packed a hearty dose of insights and wisdom into the 15 chapters of this book, I didn't want to leave out some information that's important for every believer to know. This section is filled with "Good to Know" info about the Bible, so you will be acquainted with how we got it and how we can depend on its accuracy. It also provides additional insights on key scriptures as well as a chart to assist you in choosing a translation. Be sure to check out the 22-Day Challenge, as well as the tools for using this book as a six- to eight-week group study. This bonus section is my gift to you. I hope it will enrich your love for the Scriptures and take you deeper still. Enjoy!

How Did We Get the Bible?

Throughout the centuries there have been skeptics and mockers of the Bible, and none so vehement as the French philosopher Voltaire. He applied his gift of writing in an attempt to demolish Christianity, believing that when people became enlightened they would no longer believe in God, the Scriptures, or their need for salvation through Jesus Christ. He is quoted as saying of Christ, "Curse the wretch!" Obviously Voltaire had some serious anger issues, not to mention a tad bit of arrogance. He boasted, "In twenty years, Christ will be no more. My single hand shall destroy the edifice it took twelve apostles to rear."

Voltaire died in 1778, and since his death, millions upon millions of Bibles have been printed and sold throughout the entire world. This man who said that he would expose the Bible and that it would be buried in obscurity is dead and gone, but the Word of God stands forever. Ironically, some time after his death, Voltaire's house was purchased by the Geneva Bible Society and was used as a warehouse for Bibles. The Holy Scriptures survived Voltaire, and they will continue to survive despite modern-day critics and outspoken atheists.

Jesus said, "Heaven and earth will pass away, but my words will never pass away" (Matthew 24:35). Peter described the Word as "living and enduring" (1 Peter 1:23). Isaiah penned, "The grass withers and the flowers fall, but the word of our God endures forever" (Isaiah 40:8). The Bible is an indestructible book. Many besides Voltaire have attempted to do away with it. In AD 303, the Roman emperor Diocletian issued an imperial decree that every Bible should be destroyed. Many were burned, and Christians were put to death for having them in their possession, yet this holy book endured! Even in the Middle Ages, when the Scriptures were kept from the common people, men such as John Wycliffe and William Tyndale risked their lives to translate them so all could have access through reading.

Modern-day critics of the Bible question its accuracy, and claim that it couldn't possibly be the same document as the original manuscripts. Perhaps you have wondered how we can know that it is true, accurate, and infallible. In this section we will investigate the process of how we got what we know today as the Word of God, the Holy Scriptures, the Bible. We will also look at the questions some people have about errors or contradictions. Why is it important for us to investigate the veracity of the Bible? Because it claims to be the very words of God, and if it is, then we must lean our whole life into it. It is our foundation, and we must be able to stand on it with confidence.

How Did the Bible Come Together?

The Bible has over 40 authors who were divinely inspired to write the Scriptures. Not only are the Scriptures themselves God-breathed, but we can see that God led the process by which the books were chosen. Knowing how the Scriptures came together offers beautiful evidence that God wants His people to know about His love, and He communicated His message of love through His Word.

Of course volumes could be written on the history of this amazing book, but in this section we will deal specifically with the accuracy of the manuscripts. One word we need to understand before we begin is the word *canon*, which comes from a Greek word meaning "measuring stick" or "reed." In other words, a canon was a measuring rod. The word eventually came to refer to those books that were "measured" and hence recognized as being God's Word and part of the Holy Scriptures.

The Hebrew Scriptures (which we know as the Old Testament), were written from approximately 1400 BC to 400 BC. Most of the Old Testament was recorded in the Hebrew language (with several passages in Aramaic) and was passed down by the Jewish people from generation to generation. From the time of their writing, the Jewish people accepted them as the authentic, inspired Word of God. From 400 BC to Christ's birth, several other books made their way into the popular culture of the Jewish people. These are known as the Apocrypha.* While most of the

---

* The books in the Apocrypha include 1 Esdras, 2 Esdras, Tobit, Judith, Wisdom of Solomon, Ecclesiasticus, Baruch, the Letter of Jeremiah, Prayer of Manasseh, 1 Maccabees, and 2 Maccabees.

Jewish scholars did not accept the Apocrypha as Holy Scriptures, they valued them as good literature and as sources of history and spiritual insight. Some Roman Catholic Bibles still contain the writings of the Apocrypha.

Moses, the prophets, and the other Old Testament writers were recognized by the Jews as God's messengers, and their work was accepted as inspired of God. The Old Testament canon was essentially established by the time of Jesus' birth. Around AD 90, Jewish elders met together at what is known as the Council at Jamnia, and confirmed the Hebrew canon while rejecting the books of the Apocrypha. Several years later, a Jewish historian and priest named Flavius Josephus recognized the Hebrew canon as the books that we now have in the Old Testament. Jesus quoted passages from the Old Testament, including Psalms, Deuteronomy, and Isaiah, knowing His listeners recognized these books as Scripture. By the mid-third century, the church was in almost complete agreement about the Hebrew canon of Scripture.

Old Testament Accuracy

Skeptics often criticize the Bible, saying that a book claiming to be thousands of years old certainly has inaccuracies or errors, but recent archaeological evidence again and again supports that what we have today is reliable and accurate. Looking back at the Old Testament we know that the Israelites kept the copy of the book of the Law (the first five books of the Old Testament written by Moses) inside the ark of the covenant, stored in the temple. Despite the fact that the Babylonians destroyed the temple, the Scriptures were preserved. While in Babylonian captivity certain Levites (members of the priestly tribe of Levi) began copying the Scriptures and circulating them to other Israelites in captivity.

These Levites became known as scribes, and were respected for their attention to the Scripture and their accuracy in copying them. The scribes painstakingly transcribed each copy of the Law and developed a meticulous process of copying the manuscripts by hand, in order to prevent any errors. The scribes recognized that they were handling the very Word of God and wanted to handle each word, each letter with the utmost care. Some of the rules they followed were:

- Parchments and all materials had to be made according to

strict specifications and could only come from the skins of clean (kosher) animals.

- The quills had to come from clean birds and the black ink had to be prepared to scribal specifications.

- Even if the scribe had memorized it, no word or letter could be written from memory. The scribe was required to copy every word from an authentic copy of Scripture.

- Before writing the name of God, a scribe was required to reverently wipe his pen and say, "I am writing the name of God for the holiness of His name."

- Each letter had to have space around it. If one letter even touched another or if a letter was not written correctly or defective due to a hole, a tear, or a smudge causing it not to be read easily, the scroll was invalidated.

- Within 30 days of completion, the manuscript would be reviewed by an editor who counted every letter and every word as a way of checking. The editor even made sure that the middle word of the copy matched the middle word of the original.

- Up to three mistakes on any page could be corrected within 30 days, but if more mistakes were found or if they were not fixed in 30 days, the entire manuscript had to be buried (manuscripts containing the name of God could not be destroyed). If a single letter was added or left off, the manuscript had to be fixed or buried.[1]

This careful and detailed process of copying the Hebrew Scriptures in ancient times is what has led to the accuracy of our Old Testament today. Probably one of the most significant discoveries confirming the reliability of our Old Testament Scriptures is known as the Dead Sea Scrolls. In 1947, while throwing rocks into a cave, a herdsman in Qumran near the Dead Sea accidentally discovered hidden writings of the Essene community (an ancient Jewish sect). Since that time, thousands of fragments, which belonged to more than 800 manuscripts, have been discovered.

Before these scrolls were found, the earliest known manuscript of the Old Testament was dated at around AD 980, but the Dead Sea Scrolls were estimated to date back to 150 BC! A thousand years earlier! Yet, the two sets of manuscripts are essentially the same with only a few minor variations. The scrolls include a well-preserved copy of the whole book of Isaiah and have proved to be word-for-word identical with our Hebrew Bible in more than 95 percent of the text. The remaining 5 percent is almost entirely due to spelling variations or slips of the pen. Larry Stone, author of *The Story of the Bible* (a fascinating book, by the way—a must-have) writes, "The Dead Sea Scrolls provide astonishing confirmation that the Old Testament Scripture we have today is virtually the same as that being read a few centuries before Christ. The accuracy of the transmission is remarkable!"[2]

The New Testament Canon

What about the New Testament? The process of canonizing the New Testament started during the early years of the church, as the apostles' writings were recognized as inspired and were continually read at church gatherings. Believers knew that the apostles were divinely appointed by God and gifted to communicate His message to the church. Each manuscript was handwritten (the literal meaning of *manuscript*) and very precious to the early believers. There were several reasons that a New Testament canon needed to be established. One reason was the persecution of the church. As believers faced torture, imprisonment or death for possessing the Scriptures, they needed to establish which books were sacred and worth risking their lives in order to preserve.

Also, there were spurious writings attributed to the apostles in widespread circulation throughout the first few centuries, so it was important for the early church leaders to determine which ones were divinely inspired by the Holy Spirit and should be recognized as Holy Scriptures. Although most of the books we now know as our New Testament were already being revered as Scripture, there were a few books that still needed to be examined. All along, we can see God's hand in leading the divine process of revealing Himself through the written word of the New Testament. In AD 393 at the Synod of Hippo and in AD 397 at the Synod of Carthage, Christian leaders came together to confirm the 27 books of the

New Testament. The word *synod* refers to a council or meeting of church leaders. The confirmation was not taken lightly. There were at least four general tests that were carefully used and applied to help determine the books to be canonized:

1. *Apostolicity:* Was the book's author a true apostle or closely connected to one or more of the apostles?

2. *Universality:* Does the body of Christ at large accept the book as inspired and authoritative? Was the book universally received by the church and not just by a faction?

3. *Consistency:* Does the book tell the truth about God as it is already known by previous revelation? Is the book consistent with accepted Christian doctrine?

4. *Inspiration:* Does the book's content reflect the high moral and spiritual principles that would reflect a work of the Holy Spirit? Does the book give evidence of being divinely inspired? This was the ultimate test.

The Synod at Carthage only confirmed what the church had already recognized—that these 27 books were the divinely inspired Word of God. Biblical scholar F.F. Bruce wrote,

> One thing must be emphatically stated. The New Testament books did not become authoritative for the Church because they were formally included in a canonical list; on the contrary, the Church included them in her canon because she already regarded them as divinely inspired recognizing their innate worth and generally apostolic authority, direct or indirect…What the synods of Hippo and Carthage did, was not to impose something new upon the Christian communities, but to codify what was already the general practice of those communities.[3]

Is What We Have Now, What They Had Then?

It is fascinating to see how God used the Jewish scribes to accurately preserve the Old Testament, so we can be confident in what we have today is what they had back then. We can also see His hand in preserving the New Testament. It is estimated that between 4000 and 6000 handwritten copies of the Greek New Testament have been discovered today, not to mention thousands in other languages. Some of these are entire Bibles, while others are books or pages. Some of the oldest fragments can be dated back to as far as AD 130. So the question is, How close are they to the Bible we have in our hands today?

Bible scholars and experts who have examined these ancient manuscripts conclude that although there are variations between some of the manuscripts, the vast majority of the variations are relatively insignificant, such as updated spellings, syntax, and misspellings that do not affect the original content. Only five variations have ever caused a concern, and each of these is typically noted in your Bible footnotes. And no major doctrine is in dispute in any of these variations. (The passages are Mark 16:9-20; Luke 22:20; 43-44; 23:24; and John 7:53–8:11.) Nonetheless, Bible scholars agree that what we have in our Bibles today contains in essence the same content as the early manuscripts written almost 2000 years ago.

It is exciting to see how God continues to confirm the accuracy of His Word even in modern times. From 1896 to 1906 numerous papyri manuscripts were discovered in Egypt and other sites. Papyrus comes from a river plant called *cyperus papyrus* and was specially processed to be used as a durable writing material by the ancient Egyptians. Many of the papyri discoveries contain portions of the New Testament, and these fragments have been helpful in confirming the text of other biblical manuscripts and provide information about the historical context of the New Testament. The oldest existing New Testament fragment is the John Rylands Papyrus, which dates to the period AD 125 to 150. One of the neat things about this fragment is that it lets us know that the Gospel of John was read in Egypt (far from where it was written in Asia Minor) within 50 years of John's writing of it. The Chester Beatty papyri, dating to about AD 200, are almost as old as the John Rylands Papyrus and are more extensive. They include portions of the Gospels and the book of Acts, the letters of Paul including Hebrews, and the book of Revelation.

Discoveries for both the Old and New Testaments continue to unfold. In May of 1975, workmen making repairs in St. Catherine's Monastery in the Sinai Desert discovered a walled-up room containing 70 boxes with some 3000 manuscripts. Many were nonbiblical, but there were a few leaves and fragments from Codex Sinaiticus among the discoveries. Codex Sinaiticus (originally rediscovered in 1844 by Constantin von Tischendorf) is the oldest complete copy of the New Testament, although only portions of the Old Testament survived—because monks used pages from the manuscript to light their fires in the 1800s! The Codex Sinaiticus dates back to AD 350. The word *codex* means "book." The Christians were some of the earliest writers to use the form of a book instead of scrolls. This is one case where Christians were on the cutting edge of technology!

More recently, in the summer of 2007, a team from the Center for the Study of New Testament Manuscripts (based in Dallas, Texas) traveled to the National Archive in Tirana, Albania, hoping to photograph 13 biblical manuscripts (including some dating back to the sixth century). Not only did they find the 13 manuscripts that they were looking for, but they also discovered 17 other manuscripts that were thought to be lost. They also found an additional 17 that were previously unknown to the scholarly community. They continue to discover more manuscripts all the time.* The accuracy of God's Word continues to be strengthened and confirmed with each new discovery.

As more and more biblical manuscripts are discovered, scholars are able to continue to learn more about the biblical text we study. Biblical and classical scholar Frederic Kenyon wrote, "It is reassuring at the end to find that the general result of all these discoveries and all this study is to strengthen the proof of the authenticity of the Scriptures, and our conviction that we have in our hands, in substantial integrity, the veritable Word of God."[4] My friend, if we know that this Bible we have now contains the very words of God, shouldn't we be willing to build our whole lives on it? How can we ignore or brush aside the holy words of Almighty God? Our response to knowing the accuracy of the Scriptures can be nothing less than to listen, learn, and obey.

---

* You can view some of their latest discoveries online at www.CSNTM.org. I encourage you to visit their website and see some of the photographs of early manuscripts. It's fascinating!

Bible Fact

The Gutenberg Bible is considered one of the most valuable and treasured antique books in existence. There are only 48 known to exist and of those, only 21 are complete. They are considered nearly priceless. The estimated value of a complete Gutenberg Bible between 25 and 35 million US dollars. Single pages from the book may go for as much as $25,000.

B

All About Translations

The fascinating story of how we came to have our English version of the Bible involves many brave people who risked their lives to translate the Bible into the language of the common people. As we learned earlier, the Bible was originally written in Hebrew, Aramaic, and Greek. The Old Testament was translated from Hebrew into Greek around 280 BC. This translation is called the *Septuagint* (from the Latin word for 70, which is traditionally said to refer to the number of translators who worked on the project). The Septuagint is significant for a number of reasons, but most importantly it represents one of the earliest texts of the Old Testament and is useful to scholars for understanding the original Hebrew.

Interestingly, the Greek translation of the Old Testament was quoted by the apostles in the New Testament. Yet by the fourth century AD, fewer people in the Roman Empire could speak or read Greek than had been the case in the first century, when the *koine* form of Greek had been an almost universal language. The dominant language during the 300s shifted to Latin, so there was a need for a Latin translation for the churches. In AD 382, Pope Damasus I, seeing the need for a uniform Latin translation of the Bible, commissioned a scholar named Jerome to do the work. Jerome began by revising the Gospels, using the manuscripts that were available in Greek. He used the Septuagint as his source for translating the Old Testament. By AD 400, the entire translation was complete and became known as the Vulgate, meaning in the common (or vulgar) language of the people.

From the fourth to the fifteenth century, Jerome's translation into Latin was the standard Bible used in churches. Yet, as the use of Latin began to fade out over time, the need arose again for new translations that everyone could understand. It wasn't until AD 1382 that the first Bible was translated from Latin into English. It began with Oxford scholar John Wycliffe, who recognized the importance of getting the Bible into the hands of the common people. He believed that all followers of Christ should have access to it in their own languages, but the official church organization that dominated the culture of that time believed differently. This put him at odds with the religious authorities and he risked his life to bring this new translation to the common people. Although Wycliffe began the process of translating the Bible into English (using the Latin Vulgate as his text) the work was completed by several of his associates after his death. Wycliffe's followers (called Lollards) distributed handwritten copies of the Wycliffe Bible all over England.

In 1455 the first printing press with movable metal type was invented in Germany by Johann Gutenberg. This made a revolutionary difference in producing and distributing the Bible throughout Europe. The Gutenberg Bible was a 1286-page version of Jerome's Latin Vulgate.

Another man who risked his life for the sake of the Bible was William Tyndale. Fluent in eight languages, Tyndale was an Oxford scholar and a priest. In 1525 he translated the New Testament from Greek to English, but was forced to flee England, because of the widespread rumors of his translation work. He moved to Germany and showed up at the doorstep of Martin Luther (who was translating the Bible into German). Bounty hunters and inquisitors were constantly on Tyndale's trail to arrest him and keep him from finishing the project. But God protected him and the Tyndale New Testament became the first printed edition of the Scripture in the English language. In 1535 he went on to publish part of the Old Testament, which he translated from Hebrew. In 1536, he was betrayed by someone who had befriended him (reminds you of Judas, doesn't it?), and he was taken back to England, where he was strangled and burned at the stake. His final words were "Lord, open the King of England's eyes." William Tyndale is known as the "Father of the English Bible" because his translation formed the basis of the King James Version.

A Magnificent and Mighty Work

The King James Version of the Bible has been termed "the noblest monument of English prose." King James I set the course of uniting England, Scotland, and Ireland into "Great Britain," but perhaps his crowning accomplishment was commissioning a new and improved translation of the Bible into English—one that held true to the original language of Scripture. In 1604, he appointed 54 of the world's most renowned Bible scholars and linguists to work on this accurate translation. He also wanted this to be a popular translation, so he insisted that it use old familiar terms and names and be readable in the idiom of the day.

Think about what a colossal undertaking this must have been to bring over 50 elite scholars together to translate God's Word into a readable text for a largely illiterate population. But what may seem impossible to man is possible with God. The process was a picture of providential organization. Each man who was chosen to work on the project was well-versed in Hebrew, Greek, and Aramaic languages. They were divided into six groups, and each of the groups was responsible for one section of Scripture. They used the most reliable Greek and Hebrew manuscripts available at the time. They adhered to strict rules of translation to ensure that the Authorized Version (which became known as the King James Bible in America) was a faithful translation from the original Hebrew and Greek manuscripts.

If you have ever worked on a group project in school you know that it can be frustrating if not everyone pulls their weight. Well, that wasn't the case for these scholars. Each individual in a group had to translate the same portion of Scripture as the rest of the group. Each translator tediously went through details and carefully reviewed his portion of Scripture until he felt as though he got it just right. Once the translators all worked on their portions individually, then they would come together as a group and discuss it and then choose the best of the best. As each book was completed, it was submitted to the other groups to be re-examined. You can imagine it took years to complete this project. Finally in 1611, the Authorized Version was published and is considered truly a masterpiece. Gradually more and more English translations have emerged since the King James Version was first produced.

More Help to Choose a Translation That Works for You

We learned in chapter 2 about the different philosophies and styles of translations. Here's a chart to help you get the bigger picture. On one end we have the formal equivalence versions, and on the opposite end of the spectrum we have the paraphrases.

Word-for-Word	*Thought-for-Thought*		*Paraphrase*
ASV, KJV, NKJV,	HCSB, NIV	NLT, NEB,	TLB
NASB, AMP, ESV, RSV	NET	NCV, GNT	MSG, PME
NRSV			

Formal Equivalence Translations

King James Version (KJV)

Published in 1611 (Revised in 1769)
Reading Level: Grade 12
Still strong after 400-plus years, has poetic and majestic language
and structure.

American Standard Version (ASV)

Published: 1901
Reading level: Grade 12
Considered by many to be one of the most literal, almost an
interlinear.

Revised Standard Version (RSV)

Published 1952 (revised 1971)
Reading Level: Grade 10
Was once *the* alternative to KJV; strong scholarship used in
translation.

Amplified (AMP)

Published 1965 (expanded edition 1987)
Reading Level: Grade 11
Adds more depth to key words, bringing out richness of Hebrew
and Greek languages.

New American Standard Bible (NASB)

Published: 1971 (Revised 1977, 1995)
Reading Level: Grade 11
This revision of the ASV is also an excellent literal translation of
the Bible.

New King James Version (NKJV)

Published: 1982
Reading Level: Grade 9
Is a modern reworking of KJV rather than a new translation.
Great for study, maintains poetry of King James Version.

New Revised Standard Version (NRSV)

Published: 1990
Reading Level: Grade 10
One of the more flowing, literary translations, strongly uses
gender-neutral.

English Standard Version (ESV)

Published 2001
Reading Level: Grade 10
A revision of the RSV done by evangelical scholars.

Balance Between Word-for-Word and Thought-for-Thought

New International Version (NIV)

Published 1978 (Revised 1984; major revision 2011)
Reading Level: Grade 8
Used older manuscripts of OT and NT, but very readable. Good
for memorizing.

Holman Christian Standard Bible (HCSB)

Published: 2000 (NT), 2002 (Psalms and Proverbs), 2004
(complete)
Reading Level: Grade 9
Language is clear and easy to read, and an excellent conservative
"optimal equivalent" translation.

New English Translation (NET)

Published 2005
Reading Level: Middle school
Clear and eloquent, includes translators' notes. They also offer an
online study tool at www.netbible.org.

Dynamic Equivalence

New Living Translation (NLT)

Published 1996 (Complete revision 2004; revised 2007)
Reading Level: Grade 6
Stylistically like *The Living Bible*; partially redone in 1996 by
 well-grounded biblical scholars; thoroughly redone in 2004.

New Century Version (NCV)

Published 1988 (Revised 1991)
Reading Level: Grades 5-6
Highly readable translation in today's language.

Revised English Bible (REB);
originally published as New English Bible (NEB)

Published 1989; complete revision of New English Bible (pub-
 lished 1961; NT, 1970)
Reading Level: Grade 8
Not a revision of KJV or others, rather a brand-new translation.

Good News Translation (GNT)

Published 1966 (NT); 1976 (OT); (Revised 1992); formerly
 called Today's English Version
Reading Level: Grade 8
A response to missionary requests for a Bible friendly to non-
 native English speakers as well as to the new concept of
 dynamic equivalence.

Paraphrases

The Living Bible (TLB)

Published 1971
Reading Level: Grade 4, paraphraser: Kenneth Taylor
Originally written to help author's children understand God's
 Word.

The Message (MSG)

Published 2002
Reading Level: Grade 8-9. paraphraser: Eugene Peterson
Author tried to reproduce the flavor of the original into a language that people use in everyday life.

Phillips Modern English (PME)

New Testament Published in 1958
Reading Level: Grades 6-8, translated from the Greek by J.B. Phillips
Phillips originally paraphrased this readable version for his Bible club that met in London bomb shelters during WWII. He was close friends with C.S. Lewis.

C
Overview of the Old Testament

Somethimes it helps to have a "Cliff's Notes" version to get a feel for a book in the Bible. Here's a helpful overview to give you a glimpse of each book.

The First Five Books

Genesis is the book of beginnings. Commonly believed to be written through Moses, Genesis records the creation of the universe, creation of life, the creation of the institution of marriage, and the creation of the nation of Israel. As a result of Adam and Eve's disobedience, sin is introduced into the world, but God's loving plan of redemption is also introduced (Genesis 3:15). Here we find the exciting and dramatic stories of Noah's ark, Abraham's faith, and Joseph's coat of many colors. All throughout Genesis we see the beautiful picture of God's love for His people, and His mighty hand to rescue them from disaster. Most likely written in the 1400s BC.

Exodus, which means "departure" or "going out," tells the story of God dramatically rescuing His people from their captivity in Egypt. Exodus follows their journey in the wilderness, and God's continual loving provision despite the Israelites grumbling. In Exodus we read about the ten plagues, the first Passover, and the parting of the Red Sea. The Ten Commandments are found in Exodus 20. Main characters include Moses, Aaron, Miriam, and the Pharaoh of Egypt. Penned by Moses; covers a time span from about 1526 to 1446 BC.

Leviticus could be nicknamed the "Handbook of the Priests" as it contains the instructions for worship and sacrifices. The name of the book comes from the tribe of Levi, who, along with the priests, led the Israelites in worship. The Law reminds us that we cannot get to God by means of our own righteousness. By God's grace, man is reconciled to a holy and righteous God through a blood sacrifice. Penned by Moses, it was most likely written around 1446 BC.

Numbers derives its name from the numbering of the Israelite people described within the book. We can also call it "Wilderness Wanderings," because it provides an account of the Israelites 40 years in the wilderness. It is a story about God's provision, patience, and care for His people, and offers a few warnings for us all about complaining and disobedience. Moses penned Numbers, which spans from about 1446 BC to 1406 BC.

Deuteronomy gets its name from the Greek word *deuteronomion*, which means "second law" and is Moses' farewell address to the next generation of Israelites. Moses reminds the people of God's laws and calls them to obedience as they enter the Promised Land. In this book we find the Ten Commandments presented again (Deuteronomy 5:6-21) and the story of the spies scoping out the Promised Land. It ends with Moses turning over the leadership of Israel to Joshua. Deuteronomy was written by Moses around 1406 BC.

History

Joshua is a connecting book between the Pentateuch and the historical books. This book is based on Joshua's godly and courageous leadership of the Israelites. It includes the stories of the two spies being protected by Rahab, the crossing of the Jordan River, and the battle of Jericho. God provided the victory and brought His people into the Promised Land—a lovely picture of redemption. Although the author is not explicitly mentioned, most scholars believe it was Joshua. The time period for this book is approximately 1406 to 1380 BC.

Judges is named after the "Judges of Israel," and records the fascinating stories and heroic deeds of the leaders of Israel between the time of Joshua's death and Samuel's birth. Here we discover the exciting stories of Deborah and Barak, Gideon and the Midianites, as well as Samson and Delilah. In this book we watch the Israelites go through the repeated cycle of "sin, suffering, and salvation." The book's author is unknown (some think it was Samuel). It possibly covered a span of time between 1380 BC and 1060 BC.

Ruth is the heartwarming story of a Moabite woman and her loyalty and devotion to her Hebrew mother-in-law. The book highlights God's sovereignty and care for His people as He provides a kinsman redeemer for Ruth. In the end, Ruth married her kinsman redeemer, and they had a son, Obed, who was the father of Jesse, who was the father of King David. The author is unknown (possibly Samuel again), and the events most likely occurred around 1100 BC.

The books of 1 and 2 Samuel provide a history of Israel from the last of the judges to the final years of King David. Many familiar people and events appear in these two books: Hannah, Samuel, the capture and return of the ark, Saul as the first king of Israel, David's victory over Goliath, and David's adultery with Bathsheba. Despite David's sin, we see the contrast between a man after God's own heart (David) and a man who allowed his pride to come before God (Saul). The author could possibly be Samuel, but the book includes the writings of Nathan and Gad. The events of the book occurred from about 1105 BC to 960 BC.

The books of 1 and 2 Kings offer a sequel to the books of Samuel and continue the account of the history of the Israelites. Sadly, we read of Israel's glory, division, decline, and fall—a reminder to all of us to not let the world distract us from our love of God. We meet memorable characters such as Elijah, Elisha, Ahab, and Jezebel in these books along with David and Solomon and numerous other Israelite kings. These books display both God's punishment for those who turn to idols and His power for those who turn to Him. The author is unknown (some think Jeremiah or a group of prophets) and the stories cover a time period from 960 to 560 BC.

The books of 1 and 2 Chronicles display the details of King David's reign and provide the history of Israel as well as its division and destruction. The message to be gleaned from this portrait of Israel's demise is that despite God's punishment, God still has a redemptive plan for His people, desiring to bring them back into a loving relationship with Him. In 2 Chronicles we are reminded, "If my people who are called by my name, will humble themselves and pray and seek my face and turn from their wicked ways, then will I hear from heaven and will forgive their sin and will heal their land." Certainly a message for us today! The writer is unknown but Jewish tradition indicates that it was most likely Ezra the priest. The events take place from 1000 BC to 538 BC.

Ezra could be titled, "A Fresh Start" as the Israelites had the opportunity to rebuild their nation on godly principles after about 50 years of exile. God demonstrated His faithfulness to His people by keeping His promise to restore His people to the land. Ezra, the priest, was a man who knew God's law, loved God's law, and obeyed God's law and passionately taught it to the returning Israelites. Although the author is not stated, it is generally assumed that it was Ezra, writing about the events taking place between 538 and 457 BC.

Nehemiah is one of my favorite books in the Bible. Similar to Ezra, it is about the return of the Jews from exile to build the broken walls of Jerusalem. What I love about this book is the story of God's faithful leader, Nehemiah, who sought God in every step of his challenging journey to organize the people to rebuild the walls. When God's Word was read to the people, they began to weep in repentance. Nehemiah told them not to cry, for "the joy of the LORD is your strength." The writer of this book is Nehemiah and the time of the events was about 445 BC to 430 BC.

Esther is a dramatic story that takes place in the palace of the Persian king Ahasuerus (Xerxes). We see a vivid picture of the Jews in exile and the hostility toward them. Once again God's loving plan unfolds as Esther, a Jewish girl, is chosen to be Ahasuerus's queen and risks her life to save her people. God's providential care for His people is painted throughout the story, although His name is never mentioned in the book. The author is unknown but it could have possibly been Mordecai (her cousin), or Ezra or Nehemiah. It took place between 486 BC and 465 BC.

Poetic Books

Job is a poignant reminder that bad things happen to good people, and we must guard against trying to figure out why God allows people to go through trials. In this story of one man's losses and eventual redemption, the overlying message is that we cannot understand the ways of God. The story includes not only Job's sufferings, but also a philosophical debate between his friends, and a glimpse of the heavenly interaction between God and Satan. The book doesn't give the name of the writer but the list of possible writers includes Job, Moses, Elihu, or Solomon. It is thought to have been written during the time of the Patriarchs, about 2100 BC to 1900 BC.

Psalms could be considered an ancient Jewish song book, filled with poems, praise, and heartfelt prayers. There are a variety of writers who contributed to this book, including: David (nearly half of the Psalms are attributed to him), Solomon, Asaph, Moses, Ethan, and the sons of Korah, and some don't mention an author. This collection appeals to a range of emotions dealing with life's frustrations and sorrows as well as its victories and joys. It is a reminder that we can be honest with God about our feelings and pour out our hearts to Him in worship, because of His great love for us. The date of the various writings ranges from the 1400s BC to the 500s BC.

Proverbs is a collection of wise sayings that can be practically applied to our daily lives. God loves us dearly and wants us to live with wisdom, discipline, and discernment. Proverbs encourages us to do what is right and just and fair. The first step toward wisdom is to know and revere God. Proverbs 31 includes the attributes of a wife of noble character. Solomon wrote most of the Proverbs, but there were other contributors such as Agur and Lemuel. Most likely, it was written between 970 BC and 931 BC.

Ecclesiastes reminds us of the futility of life. The writer wrestles with the age-old question, "What is the meaning of life?" and comes to the conclusion that without God, life is meaningless, empty, and unsatisfying. He sums up his quest by writing, "Fear God and keep His commands." Although the book for the most part seems depressing, if you stand back and look at the big picture you realize it is painting a picture of our need for God and the pleasure that comes from a relationship with Him. The writer is Solomon and it was probably written sometime between 970 BC and 931 BC.

The Song of Songs is a romantic story between two lovers who confess their desires for each other. It reminds us that the love between a husband and a wife is something to be enjoyed and celebrated. Commonly believed to be about Solomon and a beloved bride, it is also often interpreted as a picture or metaphor of God's love for His people or Christ's love for His bride (believers in Christ). "All beautiful you are, my darling; there is no flaw in you," reminds us in Christ we are "without blemish and free from accusation." Also known as the Song of Solomon, it was written either by Solomon or about Solomon between about 970 BC and 931 BC.

Major Prophets

Isaiah is named after the prophet who wrote it. Throughout Isaiah God is calling His chosen people back into relationship with Him. There is a two-fold message. The first 39 chapters describe God's judgment on Judah for her sins, and the second part (chapters 40–60) offers hope and comfort for the exiled people. Standing out in brilliant color is the theme that God cares for His people and will one day send a Messiah. At the beginning of Jesus' ministry here on earth, He read from the book of Isaiah and announced that He was the fulfillment of the prophecy. Written by Isaiah about the events between 742 and 681 BC.

Jeremiah was a bearer of bad news, and God's spokesman to urge God's people to turn away from their sins and turn back to Him. He stood alone with a very difficult job to carry out, and yet he shared his pain and anguish with the readers. He not only warned Judah of their coming destruction and exile, but he also saw beyond the judgment to a day when God would write His Law on people's hearts and relate to them individually in a new covenant. Although the people of Judah faced 70 years in exile because of their own rebellion, God also promised them a future and a hope. What a kind and gracious God we serve! Written by Jeremiah about the events between 626 BC and 586 BC.

Lamentations is a collection of poetic, melancholy laments of Jeremiah. Although he was the prophet to deliver the message of God's judgment on Judah and Jerusalem, he also empathized deeply with those who were suffering. God's punishment may have seemed severe, but God always brings hope. Jeremiah hoped in the unfailing love of the Lord, for His mercies are new every morning. This book reflects deep grief over sin and a humble submission to God's will, and yet turns toward the hope of God's grace and mercy. Generally believed to be written by Jeremiah (although some scholars question his authorship) around 586 BC.

Ezekiel served as both a prophet and a priest and considered himself a "watchman" for the people. His book begins with condemnation upon the people of Judah for their sin, but halfway through the book (at the fall of Jerusalem) his message turns to the suffering people, offering the hope of restoration to their homeland and one day worshipping in the temple again. Ezekiel reminds us of God's power to bring restoration even to the most dismal of circumstances. Just as God brought restoration in the Old Testament as well as at the cross, so He continues to bring restoration to our lives today. Written by Ezekiel about the events occurring from between 598 BC to 571 BC.

Daniel reminds us explicitly that God mightily rules and prevails over the affairs of individuals and of nations for His purposes. We read the exciting and faith-filled stories of Shadrach, Meshach, and Abednego as they faced the fiery furnace, as well as Daniel in the lions' den. Daniel reveals his visions, which give us a glimpse of God's plan for the ages. This book not only reminds us of God's love and power, but also inspires us to stand strong for Him in difficult times. Written by Daniel about the events ranging from 605 BC to 536 BC.

Minor Prophets

Hosea paints a magnificent picture of God's divine love for us. If you have ever questioned God's unfailing love and forgiveness, read this book. The prophet Hosea was instructed by God to marry a prostitute who was continually unfaithful, representing the unfaithfulness of the Israelites. Hosea's heart broke over the rebellion of God's people, demonstrating God's prevailing love for a people who didn't deserve it. The writer is Hosea, and it was written about the time period of 750 BC to 722 BC.

Joel offers a wake-up call to God's people that the day of the Lord is coming. There was also hope as God promised to respond in mercy to anyone who called on Him. God responds to repentant hearts that turn to Him. Joel reminds God's people that God will restore the years that the locusts have eaten—what a wonderful picture of restoration! Joel also prophesies about a day when God would pour out His Spirit on all humanity, which was fulfilled at Pentecost (Acts 2:16). Joel is the writer of this short but powerful book. The dates are unknown, but possibly occurred between 835 BC and 445 BC.

Amos was a shepherd and native of Judah, and was called by God to prophesy to the northern kingdom of Israel. The book is dominated by a message of impending judgment, yet also gives a promise of restoration to a righteous remnant in the final words of the book. Here we are reminded that God is after our hearts, and not simply rituals and festivals.

God desires a love relationship with His people! Amos wrote this book about 765 BC to 760 BC.

Obadiah is the shortest of the prophetic books with only 21 verses, yet Obadiah had a message to share: God is faithful to His people and destroys those who oppose Him. We are reminded that no matter what happens, God is in control and cares for His people. Obadiah offers the clear message that what you sow, you will also reap. Obadiah is the writer, having written around 585 BC to 550 BC.

Jonah brings us the familiar story of the prophet who ran from God and ended up in the belly of a giant fish. This book offers us many rich messages of God's grace and compassion. The overall message is that God loves everyone, even the enemies of God's people, and calls them to repentance. Jesus referred to Jonah in speaking of His own death and resurrection (Matthew 12:39). Every time I read this story God teaches me something new about Himself. The book is about Jonah, but it is not clear if it was written by Jonah or someone else, because it is written in third person. The events most likely occurred between 793 BC and 753 BC.

Micah (like Amos) condemned the hypocrisy of the religious and political leaders of his day. His message offers us all a reminder that God wants hearts that are surrendered to Him. Micah was concerned for the sinful behavior of God's people as well as the social injustice. He wept because of the impending judgment his people would face. Ultimately, God gives us the picture of true compassion as a redeeming and merciful God. Micah is the author and writes about the events around 730 BC to 686 BC.

Nahum whose name means "consolation" brings a message of comfort to his people who were being harassed by the cruel and oppressive Assyrians. He provides a vivid prediction of the destruction of Nineveh, their capital city. Nahum reminds us that God is rich in mercy, yet those who persistently refuse to accept His mercy eventually face consequences. Nahum wrote this book around 663 BC to 612 BC.

Habakkuk is a very unique book of prophesy as it begins with the prophet questioning the Lord and then moves to the Lord's response. As Habakkuk receives God's message, his doubts turn into faith as he declares, "The Sovereign Lord is my strength." The overall message is clear, trust God even when we cannot understand His ways or His timing. God is still in control of the universe, even when He allows evil to continue. It was written by Habakkuk around 600 BC.

Zephaniah reminds us that God always preserves a remnant of His people. Zephaniah's message is meant to wake up the people of God from complacency and remind them of judgment. God's message was (and continues to be), "Return to Me." One of the most beautiful portrayals of God's love is found in this book, "He will take great delight in you; in his love he will no longer rebuke you but will rejoice over you with singing." The book was written by Zephaniah around 625 BC.

Haggai is a simple and direct book calling the Jews returning from exile to wholeheartedly work on rebuilding of the temple (the House of God). He challenges the people, "Is it time for you yourselves to be living in your paneled houses, while this house remains in ruin?" He encouraged God's people to rearrange their priorities and get back to doing God's work. He reassured them that God would be with them through the whole process. What a great reminder to us as well—if God has called you to it, He will see you through it! Haggai wrote this book around 520 BC.

Zechariah offers a ray of hope and encouragement to the people of God. This book not only encourages the rebuilding of the temple, but it also reveals God's future deliverance through a coming Messiah. Zechariah predicted that the Messiah would be a victorious king, yet "humble and riding on a donkey." We also see foreshadowing of the 30 pieces of silver Judas would use to betray Jesus as well as the spear thrust into Jesus' side. This book is a reminder that God has always had a plan, leading His prophets to give inklings about Christ's coming. Zechariah was the writer of this book based on events from 520 BC to 518 BC.

Malachi warns against lukewarm faithfulness to God. The Jews were sacrificing flawed animals and had become careless in their attitudes toward God—an important reminder that God desires our whole hearts. Once again we sense the growing anticipation of the coming Messiah who will deliver His people. Malachi announces that God will send a "messenger of the covenant," who will purify Israel. He also mentions the return of Elijah, who will proclaim the day of the Lord. Malachi wrote this book about events between 460 BC and 420 BC.

Overview of the New Testament

I hope you enjoyed the snapshots of the books of the Old Testament. Here are helpful glimpses of the New Testament books. (Myself, I think these overviews are worth the price of this volume! I hope you will see it that way too.)

The Gospels

Matthew wrote his Gospel with the purpose of demonstrating that Jesus is the Messiah, the eternal King. Matthew offers the most complete account of Jesus' teachings, including the Sermon on the Mount and the parables. Matthew is the only Gospel that uses the terms *church* and *kingdom of heaven*. As Messiah, Jesus is King of a spiritual kingdom and is worthy of our praise and adoration. Written by Matthew (one of Jesus' disciples and a former tax collector) between AD 55 and 65.

Mark gives attention to Jesus' miracles showing that Jesus is the Son of God, yet this Gospel also highlights Jesus as a suffering servant. Jesus remarks, "If you want to be great in God's kingdom, learn to be the servant of all." As God's Son, Jesus came to this earth to offer His life as a suffering servant, dying on the cross for humanity's sin. God used Christ's sufferings to bring our redemption—how can we not live with gratitude for what He did for us? Written by Mark (assistant and travel companion to three early Christian leaders: Barnabas, Paul, and Peter) between AD 50 and 55.

Luke, author and doctor, traveled with Paul on his missionary travels and was considered a careful and exact historian. He showed Jesus' humanity and His compassion, and also emphasized that Jesus came to save not just the Jews, but Gentiles as well. Here we find the stories of the Good Samaritan, of the Prodigal Son, and of the rich man and Lazarus. Luke is also the only Gospel that includes the details of Christ's actual birth in Luke 2. This Gospel was written in AD 60.

John, the beloved disciple, wrote his Gospel with the purpose of conclusively proving that Jesus is the Son of God and that those who believe in Him will have eternal life. John not only recorded the events in Jesus' life, but he also related the deeper spiritual meaning. He often used words like *light, water, life, love,* and *bread.* He quoted many of Jesus' "I am" statements such as "I am the bread of life," "I am the way, the truth and the life," "I am the good shepherd." John wrote this Gospel around AD 90.

The Spreading of the Gospel / History

Acts provides us with an accurate account of the early church. In this book we read about the coming of the Holy Spirit at Pentecost and of the first Christian martyr, Stephen. We also find the story of Saul's dramatic conversion to Christ on the road to Damascus, changing his name to Paul and changing his life forever. The missionary adventures of Paul and others give us a picture of how the church grew and spread in the power of the Holy Spirit. How wonderful to know this same Spirit dwells within us as believers in Christ. Written by Luke between AD 60 and 63.

Paul's Epistles

Romans is the longest of Paul's writings and clearly teaches that all have sinned and come short of God's glory, but God has provided salvation through Christ Jesus. The first 11 chapters of Romans express and explain some of the core principles and doctrines of the Christian faith. The final five chapters of the book speak to how we should live and remind us of our own personal responsibility. Romans teaches us that we should not only know what we believe, but that this knowledge should transform our lives. Written in AD 57.

1 Corinthians is written to the Christians in Corinth, identifying problems in the church and offering solutions to living biblically in an immoral society. Paul reminds the church of the importance of personal purity and self-discipline, but most important, that love is the vital ingredient in everything we do. Paul's underlying theme throughout the letter to the church was to live in harmony with each other (1 Corinthians 1:10). Written between AD 54 and 56.

2 Corinthians defends Paul's ministry against his critics. He defends his authority as an apostle and refutes the false teachers there in Corinth. Sometimes called "the hard letter," 1 Corinthians recounts the difficulties and trials Paul and his co-workers face in the service of Christ. "Afflicted but not crushed; perplexed but not driven to despair," Paul reminds us that serving Christ may be challenging, but "God's grace is sufficient for us." Written between AD 54 and 56.

Galatians is a letter of freedom, reminding early believers that they are free from the strict Jewish laws. Once again Paul begins with doctrine in the early chapters and then progresses to the practical. He calls Christians to faith and freedom in Christ, as he reminds them to walk in the Spirit and not fulfill the lust of the flesh. Written in AD 49.

Ephesians is a beautiful reminder of all God has done for us as believers. He has adopted us, given us new life, and continues to shower us with love. Our response to such love ought to be to live a life of love for God and for others and live in obedience to Him. Paul strengthens believers as the body of Christ and tells them of the spiritual armor God has given them. Written in AD 62.

Philippians offers a message of joy and strength for believers. As Paul encourages unity among the early believers in Philippi, he reminds them of the beauty of Christ's humility and encourages them to have the same mindset. Paul thanks the Philippians for their generosity and tells them that God will supply all their needs according to His glorious riches. Paul stresses the importance of not worrying, but rather turning everything over to God in prayer. Written AD 60.

Colossians is a doctrinal letter proclaiming the Lordship of Christ. It offers one of the greatest sections of Christology in the Bible (Colossians 1:15-23). Christ is supreme over all creation. He is the image of the invisible God, and we have been reconciled to God through Christ's physical body. This is a wonderful expression of all that Christ is and all He has done for us. Paul wrote this letter to proclaim Christ's deity and to dispel false teachings. Written AD 60.

1 and 2 Thessalonians focus on Christ's return, but also emphasizes the importance of working until He comes. The church at Thessalonica faced continual persecution, so Paul also offered strength and reassurance in Christ. Paul's power-packed encouragement can be applied to our lives every day: "Rejoice always, pray continually, give thanks in all circumstances; for this is God's will for you in Christ Jesus." Written by Paul around AD 50 or 51.

1 and 2 Timothy both offer practical advice and instruction for churches as well as for believers. Paul wrote these letters to Timothy, one of his closest companions, who probably served for a time as a leader in the Ephesian church. In these epistles, Paul warns about chasing after money and instead encourages believers to be rich in good works and generous to those in need. He also encourages Timothy to not let anyone look down on him because he is young. He reminds him to "endure hardness as a good soldier of Jesus Christ." What great encouragement for us as we face difficulties in our own lives! Written by Paul between AD 62 and 67.

Titus is another "pastoral epistle" like the letters to Timothy. It instructs church leaders in their teaching and their conduct. Titus was a young church leader whom Paul had left on the island of Crete to minister to the believers there. He discusses everyday problems that a young minister may encounter and offers practical advice and guidance. Paul lists qualifications for spiritual leaders and also emphasizes that the doctrine of grace should motivate all believers to live godly lives. Written between AD 62 and 64.

Philemon is a unique short little letter in which Paul urges a slave owner (Philemon) to have mercy on a runaway slave named Onesimus. Paul encourages Philemon to accept Onesimus as a fellow brother in Christ, for he was once useless, but is now useful. A beautiful call to forgiveness, which offers a great reminder of God's grace toward each one of us. Because we are forgiven, let us live in a constant state of forgiving others. Written in AD 60.

General Epistles

Hebrews is written to help the Jews understand who Jesus is. It portrays Jesus as the great High Priest, who offered His life as the perfect blood sacrifice for our sins. Here we find the definition of faith as "being sure of what we hope for and certain of what we do not see." We are reminded that without faith it is impossible to please God, and we are given a list of great men and women of faith in Hebrews 11. The book doesn't mention an author, but early church leaders credited it to Paul. Still many scholars dispute who the author actually was, some saying it was Luke, Barnabas, or Apollos. It was written between AD 64 and 68.

James emphasizes the importance of our real faith being proven by our good works. This letter is filled with practical wisdom for daily living for believers in Christ. Listen more than you talk, know God's Word and do it, reach out to widows and orphans—to name a few. Works, not words, are the mark of a true follower of Christ. Although there are several different men who bear the name "James" in the New Testament, the James who wrote this book was most likely the half brother of Jesus and the leader of the church in Jerusalem. Written between AD 48 and 52.

1 Peter reflects the time of persecution and difficulties that the early believers were facing. Peter offered encouragement and strength and exhorted early believers to be steadfast and faithful. This first epistle of Peter's is a great reminder to us all that although life may be difficult, God will give us the strength to endure. Cast all your cares on Him because He cares for you. Written by Peter around AD 65.

2 Peter warns against false teachers and reminds believers to remain steadfast and that God will keep His promises. Peter calls the believers to live genuine godly lives and to share the good news, for Jesus could return at any time. The beautiful reminder that Peter gives us is that God has provided everything we need to live a godly life. We have received it by coming to know Christ, because of His glory and excellence we have received great and precious promises to share in His divine nature and escape the world's corruption caused by human desires! Written around AD 67.

The epistles of John (1, 2, and 3 John) reassure believers in Christ of the certainty they can have in knowing God has given them eternal life. He warns against false teachers and continues to point to both the deity and humanity of Jesus Christ. The love of God toward His children is an overall theme. Since we are loved so dearly, we must also love our brothers and sisters. Written by John the beloved apostle about AD 90 to 95.

Jude warns of heretical teachers and of their dangerous doctrines. He points to the faithlessness of the Israelites as a reminder of God's judgment. The author encourages believers to contend for the faith and commends them to the One "who is able to keep you from falling." What a beautiful reassurance that we are in God's good hands! Jude was possibly one of

Jesus' half-brothers along with James (Matthew 13:55). Written sometime between AD 65 and 80.

Apocalyptic Literature / Prophecy

Revelation was written by the apostle John while in exile on the Greek island of Patmos, and is a book that gives both warning and hope to believers. The word *revelation* in Greek is *apokalypsis*. *Apocalypse* means "disclosure or unveiling," and apocalyptic literature is filled with symbols and imagery intended to convey a message. It requires careful study and interpretation. The first few chapters are messages to seven churches in Asia Minor. Although many scholars debate how the book should be interpreted, one glorious theme is clear: the ultimate victory belongs to Christ. Written about AD 95.

E

Where to Go in the Bible for Strength and Comfort

The precepts of the LORD are right,
giving joy to the heart.
The commands of the LORD are radiant,
giving light to the eyes.

PSALM 19:8

*I*n my opinion, one of the most inspirational women in American history is Clara Barton. During the American Civil War, Clara pleaded with government leaders and army officials to allow her to enter the war zone so she could bring medical supplies and volunteer services to the wounded on the field as well as the field hospitals. One night after the battle of Cedar Mountain in northern Virginia in 1862, Clara arrived at midnight with a wagonload of supplies drawn by a four-mule team. The desperate surgeon on duty that night was completely overwhelmed by the human suffering and casualties around him. He later wrote about Clara, "I thought that night if heaven ever sent out an…angel, she must be one. Her assistance was so timely."[1]

Clara became known as the "Angel of the Battlefield" for her courageous and selfless help to the wounded and dying. I'm sure she felt inadequate at times, yet her faithfulness to bring medical supplies saved countless lives. We may never have to face a physical battlefield such as Clara did, but we do face spiritual battles every day. We are surrounded by spiritually hurting people who need to know God's love, strength, and comfort. As a former schoolteacher, Clara didn't have the medical or battlefield training to serve as a medic, but she did know where to get supplies and faithfully brought them to the wounded. Often we may feel as though we don't have the right theological training to help our wounded friends, yet we can bring healing, help, and strength to those who are weary in battle by bringing them the soothing ointment of the Word.

The Bible not only comforts and heals our hurting hearts; it also gives us strength and power to experience victory in the battles of life. In Ephesians 6, Paul reminded believers that we are not in a battle against flesh and blood, but rather, "against the rulers, against the authorities, against the powers of this dark world and against the spiritual forces of evil in the heavenly realms." That's a serious battle! Paul told us to equip ourselves with the armor of God. Most of the armor was defensive, but he wrote that we are to arm ourselves with one offensive weapon, the "sword of the spirit which is the Word of God." The Bible is our sword, our weapon in fighting life's spiritual battles.

We may not feel so strong on our own, but when we are equipped with the Word of God we have an arsenal that is able to do powerful work in the spiritual realm. Think of this section as an armory to equip you for the spiritual battles you face and to give you supplies to help others on the battlefield. You will find verses on a variety of topics so you know where to look to help a wounded warrior. I'm so thankful that Clara Barton didn't sit on the sidelines and quiver, thinking she had nothing to offer. No, she knew where the medicine was and she knew how to get it to the battlefield. May we all be spiritual "Clara Bartons," bringing life-giving supplies to those who need the inner strength that only God's Word can bring.

Reassurance of God's Love		
Deuteronomy 1:31	Proverbs 8:17	Romans 8:28
Deuteronomy 7:9	Isaiah 63:9	Ephesians 2:4-5
Psalm 37:38	Jeremiah 31:3	Ephesians 3:16-19
Psalm 103	Lamentations 3:22	1 John 3:1
Psalm 143:5,8	Hosea 2:19	1 John 4:8-11
Psalm 145:8-9	John 3:16	1 John 4:19
Psalm 145:17	Romans 5:5,8	

Help in Times of Trouble		
2 Samuel 22:30	Psalm 46:1	Romans 12:12
2 Chronicles 7:14	Psalm 86:7	2 Corinthians 1:3-4
Psalm 5:2	Psalm 121	2 Timothy 4:18
Psalm 10:14	Jeremiah 1:8	Hebrews 2:18
Psalm 18:6	Jeremiah 1:19	James 5:13
Psalm 28:7	Nahum 1:7	

Strength and Victory over Sin		
Deuteronomy 20:4	Proverbs 4:23	Philippians 4:13
Psalm 18:32	Proverbs 21:16	2 Timothy 1:7
Psalm 34:19	1 Corinthians 10:13	Titus 2:11-12
Psalm 119:45	Galatians 5:1	1 Peter 5:9
Psalm 138:3	Philippians 2:13	1 John 5:18

Turning from Anger		
Psalm 37:8	Proverbs 19:11	Ephesians 4:23
Psalm 103:8	Proverbs 21:19	Ephesians 4:26-27
Proverbs 15:1	Proverbs 25:28	Ephesians 4:31
Proverbs 16:32	Ecclesiastes 7:9	James 1:19-20

Facing Discouragement		
I Samuel 30:6	John 16:33	Romans 8:36
Psalm 62:5-7	Romans 5:5	2 Corinthians 4:16-18
Isaiah 35:3-4	Romans 8:26	2 Corinthians 12:9
Habakkuk 3:17-18	Romans 8:28	James 5:11
Mark 9:23	Romans 8:31	1 John 4:4
Luke 18:27		

Dealing with Worries or Fears		
Deuteronomy 31:8	Psalm 91:5	Philippians 4:6-7
Psalm 23:4	Proverbs 3:25-26	2 Timothy 1:7
Psalm 27:1-3	Proverbs 29:25	Hebrews 2:15-16
Psalm 34:4	Isaiah 41:10	Hebrews 13:6
Psalm 56:11	Romans 8:15	
Jesus Is God's One and Only Son—He Is Our Salvation		
Isaiah 9:6	John 8:58	Ephesians 2:13
Isaiah 53:4-6f	John 10:11	Philippians 2:5-11
Matthew 28:18	John 10:30	Colossians 1:15-23
Mark 10:45	John 14:6	1 Timothy 2:5
Luke 1:32	John 15:1-5	Hebrews 1:3
John 1:1-4	John 16:28	Hebrews 4:14
John 1:12-14	John 18:37	1 Peter 2:4
John 1:49	Romans 1:3	1 John 5:11-13
John 6:51	Romans 10:9	Revelation 1:8
John 8:12	2 Corinthians 5:14-19	Revelation 22:13-16

HELPFUL RESOURCES

- *Activating the Promises of God* by Dee Chernicky (www
  .OneHeartOneVoiceMinistries.org)
- *Counseling Through Your Bible* by June Hunt
- *Where to Find It in the Bible* by Bob Phillips

F

Miracles in the Bible

*Miracles in fact are a retelling in small letters of the very
same story which is written across the whole world
in letters too large for some of us to see.*

C.S. LEWIS

*H*ow would you define a miracle? C.S. Lewis wrote, "I use the
word Miracle to mean an interference with Nature by supernatural power." Similarly, the *Baker Theological Dictionary of the Bible*
defines a *miracle* as "an event in the external world brought about by the
immediate agency or the simple volition of God." Simply put, a miracle
is something that happens that couldn't have happened unless God were
in it. Often we try to explain away what we do not understand by trying
to give physical answers for extraordinary happenings, but if we believe
in an almighty, all-powerful God, then we also believe that He can per-
form miracles. A recent Pew Study confirms that 80 percent of Ameri-
cans believe in miracles. The Bible overflows with stories of miracles from
Genesis to Revelation.

The very first miracle we read about in the Bible is creation itself. Mate-
rialists try to explain away the miracle of creation denying that God created something out of nothing. Yet order does not come from chaos, and
the very fact that we see order in nature from the very smallest of mol-
ecules to the highest of heavens, tells me God created and ordered this
world. The Scriptures tell us that He spoke it into being, and we cannot
ignore His hand in all of creation. We may not be able to explain all of
God's methods or ways, but that does not diminish the fact that creation
itself is a miracle of God.

Other supernatural events pale in comparison to God's greatest and
grandest miracle of creation. How sad to see that so many in today's world

miss the magnificence and splendor of seeing His handiwork, dismissing it as something that "just happened." If people choose to ignore the miracle of creation, I would think it would be hard to accept the other miracles in the Bible. Either God is almighty and all-powerful, or He is not. I choose to believe the Bible. If it says it, I believe it. Each miracle shows me that I worship the High King of heaven. Nothing is too hard for Him!

Miracles in the Old Testament

Here is a list of some of the miracles we discover in the Old Testament.[1] I would encourage you to take time to do a miracle study, looking up the references and reading the stories for yourself. As you do, your faith will be bolstered, and you will be reminded of the great love God has for His people.

Old Testament Miracles	
Great flood	Genesis 7 and 8
Babel and the confusion of languages	Genesis 11:1-9
Fire on Abraham's sacrifice	Genesis 15:17
Conception of Isaac	Genesis 17:17; 18:12; 21:2
Destruction of Sodom	Genesis 19
Lot's wife turns into a pillar of salt	Genesis 19:26
Flaming bush encounter with Moses	Exodus 3:2
Moses' rod turned into a serpent	Exodus 4:3-4,30; 7:10-12
Moses' hand turned leprous and back	Exodus 4:6-7, 30
Pillar of cloud and fire	Exodus 13:21-22
Israelites' crossing through the Red Sea	Exodus 14:22
The destruction of Pharaoh's army	Exodus 14:23-30
Sweetening the waters of Marah	Exodus 15:25

Manna from heaven	Exodus 16:4-31
Quail for meat for the Israelites	Exodus 16:13
Water from the rock	Exodus 17:5-7
The plagues in Egypt	Numbers 16:46-50
Scourge of serpents	Numbers 21:6-9
Balaam's donkey talks	Numbers 22:23-30
Israelites cross through the Jordan	Joshua 3:14-17; 4:16-18
The fall of Jericho	Joshua 6:20
Sun and moon stand still	Joshua 10:12-14
Gideon's victory	Judges 6
Samson's strength	Judges 14:6; 16
Elijah and the widow's meal oil	1 Kings 17:9-16
Elijah raises widow's son	1 Kings 17:17-24
Fire on the sacrifice of Elijah	1 Kings 18:38
Many more miracles through Elijah	2 Kings 1-2
Miracles through Elisha	2 Kings 2–6
Return of the shadow on the sundial	2 Kings 20:9-11
Hezekiah's cure	Isaiah 38:21
Shadrach, Meshach, Abednego saved from furnace	Daniel 3:23-27
Daniel in the lions' den	Daniel 6:22
Sea calmed when Jonah was thrown in	Jonah 1:15
Jonah in the belly of the great fish	Jonah 1:17; 2:10
Jonah's gourd plant	Jonah 4:6-7

Miracles of Jesus

In the New Testament, the word *sign* is commonly used to represent a miracle. Just as road signs point us in a certain direction, so miracles point us in a direction as well. The signs (miracles) that Jesus performed pointed to Himself, showing that He in fact was God. The miracles Jesus performed were purposeful and significant as they confirmed to those who were looking for the Messiah, that He in fact was the One. Christ's miracles left no question of His divinity as He demonstrated not only His power to heal the sick, but also His power over creation and over evil spirits. John wrote, "While he was in Jerusalem at the Passover Festival, many people saw the signs he was performing and believed in his name" (John 2:23).

Jesus' miracles offered a turning point for many people as they placed their faith in Him. There are about 34 of Jesus' miracles recorded in the Gospels, although we know He did many others. In fact, John closed his Gospel by saying, "Jesus did many other things as well. If every one of them were written down, I suppose that even the whole world would not have room for the books that would be written" (John 21:25). I've listed all the different miracles of Jesus here in chronological order with their references in the Gospels. You will see that some are recorded in only one Gospel, while others are in three.

Jesus' miracles	
Water converted into wine	John 2:1-11
Heals the nobleman's son	John 4:46-54
Catching the fish	Luke 5:1-11
Heals the demoniac	Mark 1:23-26; Luke 4:33-36
Heals Peter's mother-in-law	Matthew 8:14-17; Mark 1:29-31; Luke 4:38-39
Cleanses the leper	Matthew 8:1-4; Mark 1:40-45; Luke 5:12-16
Heals the paralyzed man	Matthew 9:1-8; Mark 2:1-12; Luke 5:17-26

Healing of the man at pool	John 5:1-16
Restores the withered hand	Matthew 12:9-13; Mark 3:1-5; Luke 6:6-11
Restores the centurion's servant	Matthew 8:5-13; Luke 7:1-10
Raises the widow's son	Luke 7:11-16
Heals the demoniac	Matthew 12:22-37; Mark 3:11; Luke 11:14-15
Stills the storm	Matthew 8:23-27; 14:32; Mark 4:35-41; Luke 8:22-25
Throws demons out of two men of Gadara	Matthew 8:28-34; Mark 5:1-20; Luke 8:26-39
Raises Jairus's daughter	Matthew 9:18-19,23-26; Mark 5:22-24,35-43; Luke 8:41-42,49-56
Cures the woman with the issue of blood	Matthew 9:20-22; Mark 5:25-34; Luke 8:43-48
Restores sight of two blind men	Matthew 9:27-31
Heals a demoniac	Matthew 9:32-33
Walks upon Lake Galilee	Matthew 14:22-33; Mark 6:45-52; John 6:16-21
Heals the daughter of Syro-Phoenician woman	Matthew 15:21-28; Mark 7:24-30
Feeds more than 4000 people	Matthew 15:32-39; Mark 8:1-9
Restores the deaf-mute man	Mark 7:31-37
Restores a blind man	Mark 8:22-26
Heals the epileptic boy	Matthew 17:14-21; Mark 9:14-29; Luke 9:37-43
Tax money from a fish's mouth	Matthew 17:24-27

Restores ten lepers, one returns to say thank you	Luke 17:11-19
Opens the eyes of a man born blind	John 9
Raises Lazarus from the dead	John 11:1-46
Heals the woman with the spirit of infirmity	Luke 13:10-17
Cures a man with dropsy	Luke 14:1-6
Restores sight to two blind men near Jericho	Matthew 20:29-34; Mark 10:46-52; Luke 18:35-43
Fig tree withers	Matthew 21:17-22; Mark 11:12-14,20-24
Heals Malchus's ear	Luke 22:49-51
The second catch of fish	John 21:6

Matthew recorded, "Jesus withdrew from that place. A large crowd followed him, and he healed all who were ill. He warned them not to tell others about him" (Matthew 12:14-16). As a kid, I used to wonder why Jesus didn't want people to tell others. I used to think that certainly Jesus would want the news to spread about Himself as the miracle-working Messiah, but Jesus knew it was not yet His time. Although miracles were signs that attested to the fact that Jesus was in fact God, Jesus also didn't want to draw crowds who simply wanted to come see a Miracle Show.

When several of the Pharisees approached Jesus and asked for another miracle, Jesus responded, "A wicked and adulterous generation asks for a sign! But none will be given it except the sign of the prophet Jonah" (Matthew 12:38). It wasn't that Jesus didn't want to do another miracle for them. The truth is, He had already performed many for them to see, but they would not believe. He knew their hearts. One more miracle wasn't going to make them believe. Miracles can point us to Jesus, but they should never be the object of our faith or the center of our focus. Our faith is in Jesus, not the miracle.

Miracles of the Apostles

In the New Testament, we read in the book of Acts that the apostles (*apostle* means "one sent as a messenger") also performed many miracles in the name of Jesus. Again, confirming the gospel message that Jesus Christ is Lord. Here's a list of some of the miraculous events that occurred after Jesus ascended (and the ascension itself was a miracle too!).

Apostolic Miracles	
The coming of the Holy Spirit at Pentecost	Acts 2:1-4
"Signs" are done through the apostles	Acts 2:43
Peter and John heal the man lame from birth	Acts 3:1-10
Apostles prayed for boldness and signs	Acts 4:30-31
Ananias and Sapphira are struck dead	Acts 5:1-11
Apostles do many signs and wonders	Acts 5:12
Peter's shadow heals many	Acts 5:15-16
Apostles miraculously delivered from prison	Acts 5:19-23
Stephen does great signs and wonders	Acts 6:8
Philip did many signs	Acts 8:6-8,13
Saul's conversion	Acts 9:3-9
Peter heals bedridden man named Aeneas	Acts 9:32-35
Peter raises Tabitha	Acts 9:36-43
Peter miraculously delivered from prison	Acts 12:7-11
Paul strikes Elymas with blindness	Acts 13:9-11
Paul and Barnabas work signs at Iconium	Acts 14:3
Paul raises the lame man	Acts 14:8-10

Paul heals slave girl from spirit of divination	Acts 16:16-18
Paul and Silas miraculously delivered from prison	Acts 16:25-26
Paul's many miracles	Acts 19:11-12
Paul raises Eutychus to life at Troas	Acts 20:7-12
Paul saved from effects of viper	Acts 28:3-6
Paul heals Publius' father	Acts 28:7-8
Paul healed many others on the Island	Acts 28:9

As we look at these miraculous signs and wonders done through the apostles, I can't help but think of Jesus words to His disciples just before He went to the cross.

> Very truly I tell you, whoever believes in me will do the works I have been doing, and they will do even greater things than these, because I am going to the Father. And I will do whatever you ask in my name, so that the Father may be glorified in the Son. You may ask me for anything in my name, and I will do it (John 14:12-14).

What is the ultimate purpose of miracles? To bring glory to God.

When Miracles Don't Happen

To the question, "Why doesn't God answer my prayers for a miracle or for healing?" there are many possible answers. It could be something going on in the spiritual realm as with Job and Daniel. Isaiah wrote, "'My thoughts are not your thoughts, neither are your ways my ways,' declares the LORD. 'For as the heavens are higher than the earth, so are my ways higher than your ways and my thoughts than your thoughts'" (Isaiah 55:8-9). Certainly we cannot understand all of God's ways. We may not understand why God allows something to happen in our lives, but we can trust His comfort through the pain. Often we can turn around and comfort another person who is going through similar difficulties. Paul wrote,

> Praise be to the God and Father of our Lord Jesus Christ, the Father of compassion and the God of all comfort, who comforts us in all our troubles, so that we can comfort those in any trouble with the comfort we ourselves receive from God. For just as we share abundantly in the sufferings of Christ, so also our comfort abounds through Christ (2 Corinthians 1:3-5).

Sometimes God allowed people to wait for the answer to their prayers. Lazarus was sick and then died before Jesus came to his home. Why? So that God would be glorified as Jesus raised him from the dead. Another story we find in John 9 is about a man born blind. The disciples asked Jesus if the man was blind because of his own sin or was it his parents' (see, our tendency is to think all pain is a result of sin), but Jesus responded, "It was not that this man sinned, or his parents, but that the works of God might be displayed in him." Not to say there are no consequences to our sin—we know that some sicknesses or difficulties in life are a result or consequence of our disobedience to God. We also know that God takes all things in a believer's life and works it for good.

Paul wrote that his afflictions were preparing him for an eternal weight in glory beyond all comparison. He reminded believers that the things that are seen are transient, but the things that are unseen are eternal. Paul prayed three times that God would take away his "thorn in the flesh," yet it never went away. His thorn in the flesh taught him to depend on God and not on self, knowing that when he was weak, God was strong. When the miracle we ask for doesn't come, it allows us to not only lean in on God, but it also allows us to look forward to heaven. If every prayer were answered here, then we wouldn't look forward to there! Pray for miracles, trust God's wisdom, and keep your eyes toward heaven!

How to Use This Book as a
Six- to Eight-Week Group Study

*T*his is the perfect book to use in reaching out to your community or building biblical strength and wisdom in your women's group at church. If you are the leader, I encourage you to pray for your group and pray for God's direction and insight. Read through the book on your own to get a feel for how you want to lead the group. You may want to encourage the women in your group to read the chapters as homework and come prepared to discuss the questions at the end of each chapter. Use the discussion questions to get the conversation going, but then ask the women to share with the group anything they highlighted while they were reading. At the end of your study, you can encourage everyone to take the 22-Day Challenge.

Here's how *Becoming a Woman of the Word* can be broken down.

Six-Week Study	
Week One	Introduction and chapters 1 and 2
Week Two	Chapters 3–5
Week Three	Chapters 6–8
Week Four	Chapters 9–10
Week Five	Chapters 11–12
Week Six	Chapters 13–15
Seven-Week Study	
Week One	Introduction and chapters 1–2
Week Two	Chapters 3–4
Week Three	Chapters 5–6

Week Four	Chapters 7–8
Week Five	Chapters 9–10
Week Six	Chapters 11–12
Week Seven	Chapters 13–15
Eight-Week Study	
Week One	Introduction and chapter 1
Week Two	Chapters 2–3
Week Three	Chapters 4–5
Week Four	Chapters 6–7
Week Five	Chapters 8–10
Week Six	Chapters 11–12
Week Seven	Chapters 13–14
Week Eight	Chapter 15 and reflect on bonus section

Take the 22-Day Challenge

*L*ast year I invited a group of friends to join me for a 22-Day Challenge in exploring Psalm 119. This Psalm absolutely overflows with delight for God's Word. Of course, it's my hope that you will be filled with a similar excitement and love for the Scriptures as a result of reading this book. I want to encourage you to take this challenge and share in the psalmist's delight. Psalm 119 is actually an acrostic poem with 22 sections; each section starts with a letter from the Hebrew alphabet.

Here's the plan: for 22 days you will progressively read through this psalm, one section per day. Each day as you read a section, answer the following questions. You may want to use your journal for the challenge or you can write in the margin of this book. Ask some friends to join you on the challenge. It's fun and easy (won't take over five minutes of your day) and will increase your love for God and for His Word.

1. Read the section and determine what the overall theme is for the group of verses. What key words do you notice? For example in the first section (Aleph) the psalmist seems to lean toward a theme of walking in obedience. Key words are: *obey, blessed* and *ways.*

2. Use a highlighter to mark the benefits of reading and meditating on God's Word (example: will be happy and blessed, not be put to shame, and so on).

3. Underline every mention of our responsibility as the reader (example: those whose ways are blameless, walk according to the law, keep His statutes).

4. Circle each reference to God's Word or God's laws (example: statutes, precepts, ways).

5. Now insert the name of Jesus for each of the circled phrases as you read the section again. In the New Testament, John says that Jesus is the Word. He was the fulfillment of the Law and the Prophets. Write down everything you learn about Jesus as you read the passage again.

So there you have it! I know you will have a great time taking on this delightful challenge, just as my friends and I did. My hope is that you will gain wonderful insight and lasting wisdom about God, His Word, and how it affects your life. Go ahead and get started and ask a friend to join you!

Psalm 119

א Aleph

1 Blessed are those whose ways are blameless,
   who walk according to the law of the Lord.
2 Blessed are those who keep his statutes
   and seek him with all their heart—
3 they do no wrong
   but follow his ways.
4 You have laid down precepts
   that are to be fully obeyed.
5 Oh, that my ways were steadfast
   in obeying your decrees!
6 Then I would not be put to shame
   when I consider all your commands.
7 I will praise you with an upright heart
   as I learn your righteous laws.
8 I will obey your decrees;
   do not utterly forsake me.

ב Beth

9 How can a young person stay on the path of purity?
  By living according to your word.

10 I seek you with all my heart;
  do not let me stray from your commands.

11 I have hidden your word in my heart
  that I might not sin against you.

12 Praise be to you, Lord;
  teach me your decrees.

13 With my lips I recount
  all the laws that come from your mouth.

14 I rejoice in following your statutes
  as one rejoices in great riches.

15 I meditate on your precepts
  and consider your ways.

16 I delight in your decrees;
  I will not neglect your word.

ג Gimel

17 Be good to your servant while I live,
  that I may obey your word.

18 Open my eyes that I may see
  wonderful things in your law.

19 I am a stranger on earth;
  do not hide your commands from me.

20 My soul is consumed with longing
  for your laws at all times.

21 You rebuke the arrogant, who are accursed,
  those who stray from your commands.

22 Remove from me their scorn and contempt,
  for I keep your statutes.

23 Though rulers sit together and slander me,
      your servant will meditate on your decrees.

24 Your statutes are my delight;
      they are my counselors.

ד Daleth

25 I am laid low in the dust;
      preserve my life according to your word.

26 I gave an account of my ways and you answered me;
      teach me your decrees.

27 Cause me to understand the way of your precepts,
      that I may meditate on your wonderful deeds.

28 My soul is weary with sorrow;
      strengthen me according to your word.

29 Keep me from deceitful ways;
      be gracious to me and teach me your law.

30 I have chosen the way of faithfulness;
      I have set my heart on your laws.

31 I hold fast to your statutes, Lord;
      do not let me be put to shame.

32 I run in the path of your commands,
      for you have broadened my understanding.

ה He

33 Teach me, Lord, the way of your decrees,
      that I may follow it to the end.

34 Give me understanding, so that I may keep your law
      and obey it with all my heart.

35 Direct me in the path of your commands,
      for there I find delight.

36 Turn my heart toward your statutes
      and not toward selfish gain.

³⁷ Turn my eyes away from worthless things;
    preserve my life according to your word.

³⁸ Fulfill your promise to your servant,
    so that you may be feared.

³⁹ Take away the disgrace I dread,
    for your laws are good.

⁴⁰ How I long for your precepts!
    In your righteousness preserve my life.

ו Waw

⁴¹ May your unfailing love come to me, LORD,
    your salvation, according to your promise;

⁴² then I can answer anyone who taunts me,
    for I trust in your word.

⁴³ Never take your word of truth from my mouth,
    for I have put my hope in your laws.

⁴⁴ I will always obey your law,
    for ever and ever.

⁴⁵ I will walk about in freedom,
    for I have sought out your precepts.

⁴⁶ I will speak of your statutes before kings
    and will not be put to shame,

⁴⁷ for I delight in your commands
    because I love them.

⁴⁸ I reach out for your commands, which I love,
    that I may meditate on your decrees.

ז Zayin

⁴⁹ Remember your word to your servant,
    for you have given me hope.

⁵⁰ My comfort in my suffering is this:
    Your promise preserves my life.

51   The arrogant mock me unmercifully,
    but I do not turn from your law.

52   I remember, LORD, your ancient laws,
    and I find comfort in them.

53   Indignation grips me because of the wicked,
    who have forsaken your law.

54   Your decrees are the theme of my song
    wherever I lodge.

55   In the night, LORD, I remember your name,
    that I may keep your law.

56   This has been my practice:
    I obey your precepts.

ת Heth

57   You are my portion, LORD;
    I have promised to obey your words.

58   I have sought your face with all my heart;
    be gracious to me according to your promise.

59   I have considered my ways
    and have turned my steps to your statutes.

60   I will hasten and not delay
    to obey your commands.

61   Though the wicked bind me with ropes,
    I will not forget your law.

62   At midnight I rise to give you thanks
    for your righteous laws.

63   I am a friend to all who fear you,
    to all who follow your precepts.

64   The earth is filled with your love, LORD;
    teach me your decrees.

ט Teth

65 Do good to your servant
   according to your word, Lord.

66 Teach me knowledge and good judgment,
   for I trust your commands.

67 Before I was afflicted I went astray,
   but now I obey your word.

68 You are good, and what you do is good;
   teach me your decrees.

69 Though the arrogant have smeared me with lies,
   I keep your precepts with all my heart.

70 Their hearts are callous and unfeeling,
   but I delight in your law.

71 It was good for me to be afflicted
   so that I might learn your decrees.

72 The law from your mouth is more precious to me
   than thousands of pieces of silver and gold.

י Yodh

73 Your hands made me and formed me;
   give me understanding to learn your commands.

74 May those who fear you rejoice when they see me,
   for I have put my hope in your word.

75 I know, Lord, that your laws are righteous,
   and that in faithfulness you have afflicted me.

76 May your unfailing love be my comfort,
   according to your promise to your servant.

77 Let your compassion come to me that I may live,
   for your law is my delight.

78 May the arrogant be put to shame for wronging me
   without cause;
   but I will meditate on your precepts.

79 May those who fear you turn to me,
     those who understand your statutes.

80 May I wholeheartedly follow your decrees,
     that I may not be put to shame.

כ Kaph

81 My soul faints with longing for your salvation,
     but I have put my hope in your word.

82 My eyes fail, looking for your promise;
     I say, "When will you comfort me?"

83 Though I am like a wineskin in the smoke,
     I do not forget your decrees.

84 How long must your servant wait?
     When will you punish my persecutors?

85 The arrogant dig pits to trap me,
     contrary to your law.

86 All your commands are trustworthy;
     help me, for I am being persecuted without cause.

87 They almost wiped me from the earth,
     but I have not forsaken your precepts.

88 In your unfailing love preserve my life,
     that I may obey the statutes of your mouth.

ל Lamedh

89 Your word, LORD, is eternal;
     it stands firm in the heavens.

90 Your faithfulness continues through all generations;
     you established the earth, and it endures.

91 Your laws endure to this day,
     for all things serve you.

92 If your law had not been my delight,
     I would have perished in my affliction.

93 I will never forget your precepts,
for by them you have preserved my life.

94 Save me, for I am yours;
I have sought out your precepts.

95 The wicked are waiting to destroy me,
but I will ponder your statutes.

96 To all perfection I see a limit,
but your commands are boundless.

מ Mem

97 Oh, how I love your law!
I meditate on it all day long.

98 Your commands are always with me
and make me wiser than my enemies.

99 I have more insight than all my teachers,
for I meditate on your statutes.

100 I have more understanding than the elders,
for I obey your precepts.

101 I have kept my feet from every evil path
so that I might obey your word.

102 I have not departed from your laws,
for you yourself have taught me.

103 How sweet are your words to my taste,
sweeter than honey to my mouth!

104 I gain understanding from your precepts;
therefore I hate every wrong path.

נ Nun

105 Your word is a lamp for my feet,
a light on my path.

106 I have taken an oath and confirmed it,
that I will follow your righteous laws.

107 I have suffered much;
　　　preserve my life, LORD, according to your word.

108 Accept, LORD, the willing praise of my mouth,
　　　and teach me your laws.

109 Though I constantly take my life in my hands,
　　　I will not forget your law.

110 The wicked have set a snare for me,
　　　but I have not strayed from your precepts.

111 Your statutes are my heritage forever;
　　　they are the joy of my heart.

112 My heart is set on keeping your decrees
　　　to the very end.

ס Samekh

113 I hate double-minded people,
　　　but I love your law.

114 You are my refuge and my shield;
　　　I have put my hope in your word.

115 Away from me, you evildoers,
　　　that I may keep the commands of my God!

116 Sustain me, my God, according to your promise, and I will live;
　　　do not let my hopes be dashed.

117 Uphold me, and I will be delivered;
　　　I will always have regard for your decrees.

118 You reject all who stray from your decrees,
　　　for their delusions come to nothing.

119 All the wicked of the earth you discard like dross;
　　　therefore I love your statutes.

120 My flesh trembles in fear of you;
　　　I stand in awe of your laws.

ע Ayin

121 I have done what is righteous and just;
    do not leave me to my oppressors.

122 Ensure your servant's well-being;
    do not let the arrogant oppress me.

123 My eyes fail, looking for your salvation,
    looking for your righteous promise.

124 Deal with your servant according to your love
    and teach me your decrees.

125 I am your servant; give me discernment
    that I may understand your statutes.

126 It is time for you to act, LORD;
    your law is being broken.

127 Because I love your commands
    more than gold, more than pure gold,

128 and because I consider all your precepts right,
    I hate every wrong path.

פ Pe

129 Your statutes are wonderful;
    therefore I obey them.

130 The unfolding of your words gives light;
    it gives understanding to the simple.

131 I open my mouth and pant,
    longing for your commands.

132 Turn to me and have mercy on me,
    as you always do to those who love your name.

133 Direct my footsteps according to your word;
    let no sin rule over me.

134 Redeem me from human oppression,
    that I may obey your precepts.

135 Make your face shine on your servant
    and teach me your decrees.
136 Streams of tears flow from my eyes,
    for your law is not obeyed.

צ Tsadhe

137 You are righteous, LORD,
    and your laws are right.
138 The statutes you have laid down are righteous;
    they are fully trustworthy.
139 My zeal wears me out,
    for my enemies ignore your words.
140 Your promises have been thoroughly tested,
    and your servant loves them.
141 Though I am lowly and despised,
    I do not forget your precepts.
142 Your righteousness is everlasting
    and your law is true.
143 Trouble and distress have come upon me,
    but your commands give me delight.
144 Your statutes are always righteous;
    give me understanding that I may live.

ק Qoph

145 I call with all my heart; answer me, LORD,
    and I will obey your decrees.
146 I call out to you; save me
    and I will keep your statutes.
147 I rise before dawn and cry for help;
    I have put my hope in your word.
148 My eyes stay open through the watches of the night,
    that I may meditate on your promises.

149 Hear my voice in accordance with your love;
    preserve my life, LORD, according to your laws.

150 Those who devise wicked schemes are near,
    but they are far from your law.

151 Yet you are near, LORD,
    and all your commands are true.

152 Long ago I learned from your statutes
    that you established them to last forever.

ר Resh

153 Look on my suffering and deliver me,
    for I have not forgotten your law.

154 Defend my cause and redeem me;
    preserve my life according to your promise.

155 Salvation is far from the wicked,
    for they do not seek out your decrees.

156 Your compassion, LORD, is great;
    preserve my life according to your laws.

157 Many are the foes who persecute me,
    but I have not turned from your statutes.

158 I look on the faithless with loathing,
    for they do not obey your word.

159 See how I love your precepts;
    preserve my life, LORD, in accordance with your love.

160 All your words are true;
    all your righteous laws are eternal.

ש Sin and Shin

161 Rulers persecute me without cause,
    but my heart trembles at your word.

162 I rejoice in your promise
    like one who finds great spoil.

163 I hate and detest falsehood
     but I love your law.

164 Seven times a day I praise you
     for your righteous laws.

165 Great peace have those who love your law,
     and nothing can make them stumble.

166 I wait for your salvation, LORD,
     and I follow your commands.

167 I obey your statutes,
     for I love them greatly.

168 I obey your precepts and your statutes,
     for all my ways are known to you.

ת Taw

169 May my cry come before you, LORD;
     give me understanding according to your word.

170 May my supplication come before you;
     deliver me according to your promise.

171 May my lips overflow with praise,
     for you teach me your decrees.

172 May my tongue sing of your word,
     for all your commands are righteous.

173 May your hand be ready to help me,
     for I have chosen your precepts.

174 I long for your salvation, LORD,
     and your law gives me delight.

175 Let me live that I may praise you,
     and may your laws sustain me.

176 I have strayed like a lost sheep.
     Seek your servant,
     for I have not forgotten your commands.

Notes

Introduction—Anything but Boring

1. Jim Denison, Denison Forum on Truth and Culture, www.Denisonforum.org, January 20, 2014 entry.

Chapter 1—Invitation to Dine

1. http://solutionsforyourlife.ufl.edu/hot_topics/families_and_consumers/family_dinners.html.
2. Andrew Murray, *The Spirit of Christ* (New Kensington, PA: Whitaker House, 1984), pp. 78-80.
3. Go to www.OnCallPrayer.org to find out more.
4. L.B. Cowman, comp., *Streams in the Desert* (Grand Rapids, MI: Zondervan, 1997), p. 414.

Chapter 2—Daily Swim

1. www.ligonier.org/blog/get-basic-overview-bible/.

Chapter 3—Diving Deeper

1. Corrie ten Boom, *Each New Day* (Grand Rapids, MI: Fleming H. Revell Company, 1977), August 21 entry.

Chapter 4—Breathe It In

1. Don Postema, *Space for God* (Grand Rapids, MI: Faith Alive Christian Resources, 1997), p. 104.
2. Dietrich Bonhoeffer. *Meditating on the Word* (Lanham, MD: Cowley Publications, 1985), p.30.

Chapter 5—Never Go Anywhere Without It

1. Warren W. Wiersbe, *50 People Every Christian Should Know* (Grand Rapids, MI: Baker Books, 2009), p. 159.
2. www.wholesomewords.org/biography/bhavergal3.html.
3. Chuck Swindoll, "Seeing the World through God's Eyes," *Insights*, April 2008, accessed April 2013, www.insightforliving.ca/insights/think-jesus/seeing-the-world-through-gods-eyes.html.

Chapter 6—The Big Picture

1. Henri Nouwen, *The Return of the Prodigal Son* (New York: Doubleday Publishers, 1992), p. 5.
2. Nouwen, p. 43.

Chapter 7—God's Favorite Color

1. Andrew Murray, *The Power of the Blood of Jesus* (New Kensington, PA: Whitaker House, 1993), p. 12.

Chapter 8—Covenant of Love

1. Vern S. Poythress, "Overview of the Bible: A Survey of the History of Salvation," article in *English Standard Version Study Bible* (Wheaton, IL: Crossway Publishers, 2008), p. 24.

Chapter 9—You Are Never Alone

1. Andrew Murray, *Experiencing the Holy Spirit* (New Kensington, PA: Whitaker House, 1985), p. 13.

2. www.monergism.com/thethreshold/articles/onsite/packer_regen.html.

3. www.monergism.com/thethreshold/articles/onsite/packer_regen.html.

Chapter 10—Seven Loving Words

1. John Stott, as quoted in *More Gathered Gold,* ed. John Blanchard (Hertfordshire, England: Evangelical Press, 1986), p. 181.

2. www.ligonier.org/blog/what-sanctification/.

3. Harry Foster, as quoted in *More Gathered Gold*, p. 126.

Chapter 11—How to Have Zero Impact in the World

1. Michael Catt, *Courageous Living: Dare to Take a Stand* (Nashville, TN: 2011).

Chapter 12—Fully Engaged

1. Francis Schaeffer, *The Mark of the Christian* (Westmont, IL: InterVarsity Press, 1976), p. 15.

2. Steve Corbett and Brian Fikkert, *When Helping Hurts* (Chicago: Moody Publishers, 2009), p. 74.

Chapter 13—Pray-pared for Each Day

1. C.H. Spurgeon, *Morning and Evening* (Grand Rapids, MI: Zondervan, 1955), p. 31.

2. http://thirtyeightfive.com/2014/01/08/a-call-to-prayer/#comments.

Chapter 14—The Heart of Worship

1. http://metro.co.uk/2013/12/14/hope-for-paws-miley-video-abandoned-dog-on-rubbish-tip-makes-amazing-recovery-4230505/.

2. Geoffrey B. Wilson, as quoted in *More Gathered Gold*, ed. John Blanchard (Hertfordshire, England: Evangelical Press, 1986), p. 345.

Chapter 15—Church Redefined

1. *Strong's Greek Dictionary of the New Testament,* p. 81.

2. Charles Clayton Morrison, *What Is Christianity?* (Chicago: Willett, Clark and Co.), p. 108.

3. Erik Thoennes, "Biblical Doctrine: An Overview," article in *English Standard Version Study Bible* (Wheaton, IL: Crossway Publishing, 2008), p. 2532.

4. Ernest Southcott, as quoted in Neil Hunter, "Going 'to' Church, or 'Being' the Church?" www.mosaic-nc.org/going-to-church-or-being-the-church.

5. *More Gathered Gold,* ed. John Blanchard (Hertfordshire, England: Evangelical Press, 1986), p. 49.

6. http://neverstoplearning1.blogspot.com/ Wednesday, December 14, 2005.

A—How Did We Get the Bible?

1. Larry Stone, *The Story of the Bible* (Nashville, TN: Thomas Nelson Publishers, 2010), p. 21.

2. Stone, p. 27.

3. F.F. Bruce, *The New Testament Books: Are They Reliable?* (Grand Rapids, MI: William B. Eerdmans Publishing Co., 1981), p. 22.

4. Frederic Kenyon, *The Story of the Bible* (London: John Murray Publishers, 1935), p. 113.

E—Where to Go in the Bible for Strength and Comfort

1. www.redcross.org/about-us/history/clara-barton.

F—Miracles in the Bible

1. This is a partial list of Old Testament miracles. For a complete list I suggest using *Nave's Topical Study Bible* as a resource.

About the Author

Karol Ladd is known as the "Positive Lady." Her unique gift of encouraging women from the truths of God's Word, as well as her enthusiasm and joy, is evident in both her speaking and her writing.

Karol is the bestselling author of over 35 books, including *Positive Life Principles for Women* and *Positive Leadership Principles for Women, The Power of a Positive Mom,* the devotional *Pursuing God in the Quiet Places, Unfailing Love* (1 John), *A Woman's Passionate Pursuit of God* (Philippians), and *A Woman's Secret to Confident Living* (Colossians). She is a gifted Bible teacher and popular speaker to women's organizations, church groups, and corporate events across the nation. Karol is also a frequent guest on radio and television, sharing a message of joy and strength found in the Lord. Her most valued role is that of wife to Curt and mother to daughters Grace and Joy.

Visit her website at www.PositiveLifePrinciples.com for daily doses of encouragement and more information on how you can start your own Positive Woman Connection Bible Study.

Also by Karol Ladd

Positive Life Principles for Women
8 Simple Secrets to Turn Your Challenges into Possibilities

What woman doesn't sometimes feel like her life is "slightly imperfect"...maybe even over-the-top imperfect?

Karol Ladd looks at the not-so-perfect lives of eight women in the Bible to show you how to turn your challenges and blunders into possibilities for growth, change, and maturity. Eight powerfully effective chapters give you encouragement to

- *listen to the right voices,* shown by the life of Eve
- *guard against comparisons,* exemplified in the life of Sarah
- *reach out and help others,* demonstrated in the life of Ruth

You'll see how to learn from your mistakes and become stronger despite adversity...and find hope, refreshment, and renewal for your "slightly imperfect" life.

Positive Leadership Principles for Women
8 Secrets to Inspire and Impact Everyone Around You

As a woman you have the chance to make a positive difference in your family, your community—even your society. In this dynamic resource, Karol Ladd offers positive, motivating words to women in leadership and those who need or want to be. Karol highlights eight godly leadership principles and attitudes that you can build into your life now, such as

- *rising to the challenge*—shown in the life of Joseph
- *taking calculated risks*—exemplified in the leadership of Deborah
- *inspiring passion in others*—displayed in Nehemiah's attitude

Wherever your opportunity lies as a leader, you'll be inspired to grow in your role as a godly influencer—leading and motivating others toward God's love and maturity in the faith.

Unfailing Love
A Woman's Walk Through First John

It's easy to talk about filling your heart with God's love, but it's another thing to embrace His love, feel it, and allow it to color the fabric of your life. In this insightful journey through 1 John, Karol Ladd invites you to experience the reality of God's generous love. As you begin to grasp its height and depth…

- you're transformed, seeing yourself and your circumstances in a fresh new light.

- you get a truer picture of Jesus, God's Son, in a way that helps you navigate the false loves, temporary pleasures, and seductions of today's culture.

- you're able to graciously, compassionately, and creatively love others by your words and actions.

A Woman's Passionate Pursuit of God
Creating a Positive and Purposeful Life

As you explore Paul's intriguing letter to the Philippians with Karol Ladd, you'll learn to live intentionally as you face life's daily challenges. Most important, you'll be helped to understand God's Word and His plans for your life and say more and more, "Father, I want what You want."

Filled with inspiring true-life stories, practical steps, and study questions, this book is perfect for personal quiet times, a book club pick, or a group Bible study.

A Woman's Secret for Confident Living
Becoming Who God Made You to Be

Karol Ladd shares powerful truths from the book of Colossians to help you make a vital shift in perspective. Knowing Christ and His greatness, and knowing who you are in Him, sets you on an exciting path to living—not in self-confidence, but *God*-confidence. You'll be helped to

- get rid of negative and self-defeating thoughts

- cultivate your potential, because you're valuable to Him
- shine with joy and assurance of what you bring to the world

Includes questions to bring depth and dimension to individual or group study.

More to Help You Experience the Bible

The Daily Bible®
With Devotional Insights to Lead You Through God's Word
Commentary by F. LaGard Smith

Unlike any other Bible you have read, this bestselling chronological presentation of God's story unfolds in front of you daily, helping you begin to appreciate God's plan for your life as never before. Reading the Bible will become a fresh, inviting, more informative experience. *The Daily Bible*'s 365 convenient segments offer...

- the highly readable New International Version...the most popular modern version of Scripture
- chronological/historical arrangement of every book of the Bible, which lets you easily understand God's redemptive plan as you read from creation to Revelation
- unique devotional commentary that leads you smoothly through Scripture, painting the scene for what is about to be read with historical and spiritual insights

E-book, softcover, hardcover, as well as large print—the *Daily Bible* is available in an edition to suit your needs and preferences.